MICROSOFT EX

A PRACTICAL AND EFFECTI
MICROSOFT EXCEL 2022, LEARN THE ESSENTIAL
FUNCTIONS, NEW FEATURES, FORMULAS, TIPS AND
TRICKS, AMAZING TOOL OF EXCEL, AND UTILIZE THEM AT
YOUR WORKPLACE

Table of Contents

Introduction

Microsoft Excel is a spreadsheet program for managing and organizing numerical and statistical data. Microsoft Excel includes a variety of tools for performing tasks such as calculations, pivot tables, graphing tools, macro programming, and more. It works for a variety of operating systems, including Windows, Mac OS X, Android, and iOS.

This Guidebook compiles all of the required information for utilizing the current version of Microsoft Excel's many functionalities. This book strives to be of help to all users, regardless of what and how experience they have with the software. It is written in a straightforward, easy-to-understand manner.

Excel's greatest strength is that it can be used for a wide range of business activities, such as finance, forecasting, statistics, data management, business intelligence, billing and inventory tracking, and analysis. Spreadsheets are familiar to someone who is using a device for anything than just playing games. A spreadsheet is multi-functional programming software (package) that allows you to do dynamic calculations and generate best charts and graphs.

Fortunately, learning Excel is well worth the effort since it is unquestionably one of the greatest analysis tools and data-processing ever devised. Microsoft Excel is certainly the most common data management tool used by nearly anyone in the world. Excel is used with too great success and value for nearly every organization. Excel is an unbelievably efficient way to gain value from huge quantities of info. It works well, however, to calculate and monitor almost every kind of detail. The cell grid can unlock all this ability. Numbers, text or formulas can be used in cells. You insert and organize the data in columns and rows in your cells. You can install, sort, filter, place it in tables and make amazing charts. It helps you to add the information.

The purpose of this book is to expose you to Microsoft Excel when you do not know much about it. The concepts in this book take you to the basics of developing and using Excel tables, graphics, etc.

Implementing development programs so that workers can remain on top of the newest technology and work as effectively as possible is one approach to remain ahead of the pack and enhance profitability. Employers may also preserve one of their most significant assets: their people via ongoing training and growth. MS Excel helps the employees that are talented and desire to be motivated and work hard to remain ahead of the competition who must have the advanced knowledge of new software and technologies.

This Excel Guide compiles all of the required how-to information for utilizing the current version of Microsoft Excel's many functionalities. This book strives to be of help to all users, regardless of what and how experience they have with the software. It is written in a straightforward, easy-to-understand manner.

This book is written to expose you to the rudiments of excel in an evolving economy where virtually all transactions are based on the power of the internet. But you cannot handle fiscal transactions accurately without tools such as Microsoft Excel. Let's get started.

Chapter 1: Understanding Microsoft Excel

What is Excel?

Microsoft Excel is a spreadsheet program for Windows, Android, macOS, and iOS that was created by Microsoft. It is a database application used primarily for recording and analysing numerical results. Consider a spreadsheet to be a table made up of columns and rows. Columns are normally allocated alphabetical characters, while rows are typically assigned numbers. A cell is the intersection of a column and a row.

As an example, all individuals work with numbers in some way. They all have regular bills that they compensate for from monthly earnings. To invest wisely, one must first understand their revenue and spending. When one needs to log, analyse, and store numeric details, Excel comes in handy.

Microsoft Excel is used in a variety of formats. It's available from a computer hardware store that also offers applications. Microsoft Excel is a software that is merely a fragment of the Microsoft Office suite. You can even get it from the Microsoft store, although you'll have to pay for the license key.

In today's complex business climate, custom solutions are required to maintain a competitive edge and optimize revenues.

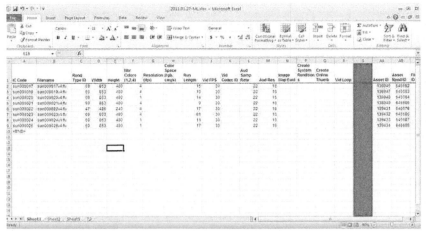

The most experienced in new and evolving developments are Microsoft Excel consultancy companies. Having a dedicated professional expert on retainer is vital to reaching the optimum strength and productivity required to excel in the twenty-first century. You can contact them right away, whether you need Excel solutions or preparation.

Historical background of excel

Microsoft Excel is a spreadsheet program created by Microsoft Corporation in 1985. Excel is a widely used spreadsheet program that organizes the data in rows and columns, which can be edited using formulae to perform the mathematical operations on data.

1, 2 & 3 Lotus, initially released in 1982 by Lotus Development Corporations, dominated the mid-1980s spreadsheets market for the PCs or personal computers running Microsoft's MS-DOS operating system. Microsoft created a rival spreadsheet, & the 1st version of Excel for Apple Inc.'s Macintosh computer was published in 1985. The new program soon gained popularity due to its excellent visuals and speedy processing. Excel was able to establish a following among Macintosh users since 1, 2 & 3 Lotus wasn't available for Macintosh. In 1987, Microsoft released another version of Excel, which was the first to operate on the company's new Windows operating systems. The powerful application gained popularity because of its graphics-heavy interface, which was built to operate on the newest Windows systems. Lotus took a long time to create Windows versions of the spreadsheet, enabling Excel to gain market dominance and finally overtake Lotus as the most popular spreadsheet program in the mid-1990s. Toolbars, outlining, sketching, 3D charts, various shortcuts, & more automated functions were all included in later versions of Excel. Microsoft updated the naming scheme for Excel in 1995 to highlight the product's first release year. 95 Excel was created for the newest Intel Corporation 386 microprocessor-based 32-bit systems. Excel 97 In 1997 and Excel 99 in 1999 (, new versions were released (Excel 2000). 2002 Excel was introduced in 2003 as part of the Office XP package, and it introduced a major new feature that enabled users to restore Excel data in the case of computer breakdown.

Excel 2007 included a revamped user interface that shared functionality with Microsoft's Word & PowerPoint programs, enabling users to navigate seamlessly between them. Additionally, data sharing, chart creation, security, sorting, formula writing, and filtering have all been enhanced.

How Excel Works

A Workbook is a name given to an Excel document. Worksheets are always present in a workbook. Worksheets are a grid for storing and calculating data. A workbook may include a large number of worksheets, each with its own name.

Worksheets are organized into columns (vertical) and rows (horizontal) (horizontal). A cell is a point where any two rows and columns meet. Cells are where you input all of your data. You may type a lot of text in a cell, or you may input a date, number, or formula. Each cell may be customized with its own border, background color, and font color, size, and type.

Terms used in Microsoft Excel

There are some terms in Excel which I want you to know about. Knowing about these terms will make your learning easy. It will save you the time of making extra research to find the meaning of some keywords you may not understand.

Button

A button simply implies an icon you can click on in Excel to complete specific task. Different buttons are used for different task completion. Buttons include bold, underline, text align, and others. In Excel program, button can be called **command or tool**. Buttons are just those designs in any application which you can click to get any specific job done.

Workbook

The term workbook means a collection of cells organized in rows and columns. It is that working surface you will interact with when you start making use of your Excel application. It is that spreadsheet where you enter texts and numbers. A workbook can contain many spreadsheets inside of it.

Spreadsheet

The word spreadsheet means a working environment in Excel where you can enter your data in different cells. A spreadsheet is also called worksheet or sheet.

Copy, Cut, and Paste

In many Microsoft application products, copy, cut and paste are commonly used words. In Microsoft Word for instance, they are common actions taken by users. I will like to explain the terms for you. When you select text or right-click any cell in Excel, you will be shown cut, copy and paste among other options.

If you click *cut*, the text or number will be deleted from the cell and you can paste it in another cell in the spreadsheet. When you select *copy,* the text or number will be copied in the computer clipboard and remains in the cell, and you can paste it in another cell.

To paste implies to place the current content of your computer clipboard (the copied text or number) in another cell of the spreadsheet.

Row

Row is a common term in Mathematics study. I started hearing of it right from my primary school days. In Excel, a row is the horizontal section of the spreadsheet containing many cells. It is made up of cells arranged horizontally. Rows in Excel are numbered.

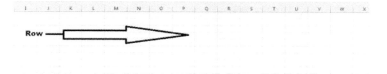

The direction of row shown

Column

Just like row, column was a common term to me in my primary school days especially in Statistics. A column is the vertical line of cells of Excel spreadsheet. It involves cells arranged in vertical order. Columns are labelled in letters.

Cell

A cell is the building block of Excel program. It is a location at the intersection of a particular row and column. Depending on the size an Excel user chooses for cells, they can be rectangular or square in shape. Without cells, there is nothing like Excel application. They are where values including texts are entered in the spreadsheet.

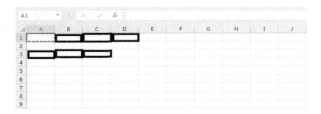

Picture indicates some cells in rectangular shape

Data

In this book, I will be using the term *data* frequently to make my teaching. In this teaching, data are texts, numbers, or even icons. When I say prepare your data anywhere in this teaching, I mean you should prepare your information in Excel sheet which you will use to create chart or complete a particular task.

Where Is Excel Used

1. Calculating

By programming your frequently used formulae in Excel, you may create a completely personalized calculator. That way, all you have to do is type in your numbers, and Excel will calculate the result for you—no effort necessary.

2. Accounting

Budgeting, forecasting, cost monitoring, financial reports, loan calculators, and other tools are all available. Excel was essentially created to fulfill these various accounting requirements. And, given that 89 percent of businesses use Excel for different accounting duties, it clearly meets the criteria.

3. Charting

The collection of scatter charts, bar charts, pie charts, line charts, column charts and area charts is endless. Excel's ability to turn rows and columns of figures into attractive charts is likely to become one of your favorite features if you want to convey data in some more visual and consumable manner.

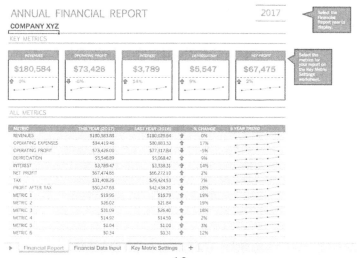

4. Inventory tracking

Budget

% of Income Spent Summary

Total Monthly Income
$3,750
Total Monthly Expenses
$2,058
Total Monthly Savings
$550
Cash Balance
$1,142

55%

Inventory management may be a pain. Fortunately, Excel can assist workers, company owners, and even individuals in staying organized and on top of their inventory before big issues arise.

Personal Inventory

Name	Insurance Company	Agent Address
[Name]	[Company]	[Address]
Address	Agent	Agent Phone
[Address]	[Name]	[Phone/Fax]
Phone	Company Phone	Agent Email
[Phone]	[Phone]	[Email]
Email	Policy Number	
[Email]	[Policy]	

Item Description	Category	Serial Number	Value
[Item]	[Category]	[Serial #]	[Value]
[Item]	[Category]	[Serial #]	[Value]
[Item]	[Category]	[Serial #]	[Value]
[Item]	[Category]	[Serial #]	[Value]
[Item]	[Category]	[Serial #]	[Value]
[Item]	[Category]	[Serial #]	[Value]
[Item]	[Category]	[Serial #]	[Value]
[Item]	[Category]	[Serial #]	[Value]
Total			$0.00

5. Calendars and schedules

Do you need to create a content schedule for your blog or website? Are you looking for lesson ideas for your classroom? Is there a PTO schedule for you and your coworkers? Do you or your family have a daily schedule? Excel may be surprisingly powerful when it comes to multiple calendars.

6. Seating charts

Creating a seating plan for anything from a major business lunch to a wedding may be a royal hassle. Excel, fortunately, can make it a breeze. If you're a true wiz, you'll be able to build your seating chart automatically from your RSVP spreadsheet.

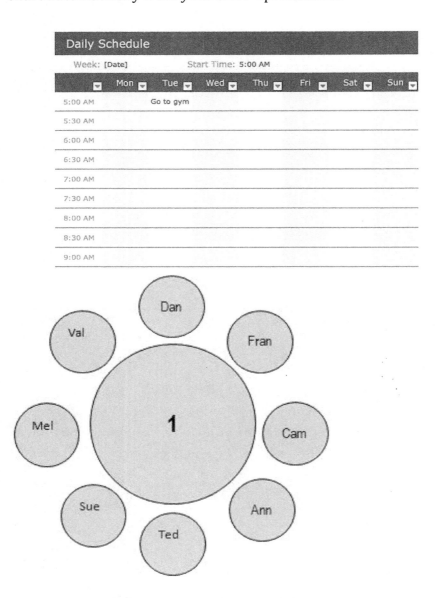

7. Goal planning worksheet

Excel's beauty is shown. You may use the tool to build a variety of spreadsheets, logs, and planning papers to track your progress.

Task	Times/Week	S	M	T	W	T	F	S	Complete
Go for a run	2	✔		✔					Yay!
Don't Leave Dirty Dishes Overnight	2	✔			✔		✔		Yay!
Eat 1 Fruit or Vegetable	3	✔			✔	✔	✔	✔	Yay!
Floss	3	✔		✔			✔	✔	Yay!

8-3-2014									
Task	Times/Week	S	M	T	W	T	F	S	Complete
Go for a run	2								0 of 2
Don't Leave Dirty Dishes Overnight	3								0 of 3
Eat 1 Fruit or Vegetable	3								0 of 3
Floss	3								0 of 3

8-10-2014									
Task	Times/Week	S	M	T	W	T	F	S	Complete
Go for a run	3								0 of 3
Don't Leave Dirty Dishes Overnight	3								0 of 3
Eat 1 Fruit or Vegetable	4								0 of 4
Floss	4								0 of 4

8-17-2014									
Task	Times/Week	S	M	T	W	T	F	S	Complete
Go for a run	3								0 of 3
Don't Leave Dirty Dishes Overnight	3								0 of 3
Eat 1 Fruit or Vegetable	5								0 of 5
Floss	4								0 of 4

8. Mock-ups

When it comes to design, Excel may not be the first thing that springs to mind. However, believe it or not, the tool may be used to create numerous mock-ups and prototypes. It's a popular option for developing website wireframes and dashboards, in fact.

Getting stuff done

Do you want to increase your productivity? Excel, on the other hand, may come to your rescue with a range of functions that may help you manage your chores and to-dos with simplicity and order.

9. Tasklist

Say goodbye to your old-fashioned to-do list on paper. With Excel, you can create a far more comprehensive worklist—and even

monitor your progress on the bigger tasks you presently have on
your plate.

TASK LIST					
MY TASKS	START DATE	DUE DATE	% COMPLETE	DONE	NOTES
[Task]	[Date]	[Date]	0%		
[Task]	[Date]	[Date]	50%		
[Task]	[Date]	[Date]	100%	●	

10. Checklist

Similarly, you may make a basic checklist to cross off the items
you've bought or completed—from a shopping list to a list of to-
dos for a planned marketing campaign.

11. Project management charts

Excel is a real beast when it comes to making charts, as we've
previously said. This principle is also valid when it comes to
different project management charts.

Excel can help you keep your project on schedule in a variety of
methods, from waterfall charts to kanban style boards (much like
Trello!) to oversee your team's progress.

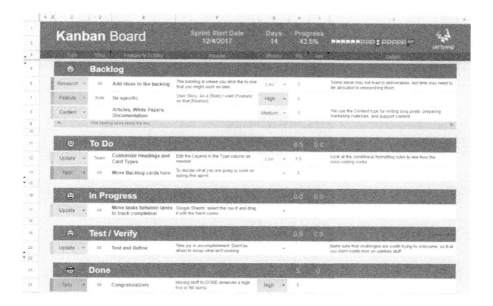

12. Time logs

You already know that keeping track of your time may help you be more productive. At the same time, there are many sophisticated applications and tools to assist you in satisfying that demand; consider Excel as the original time-tracking tool. It continues to be a viable alternative today.

Time Sheet

[Employee name] | [Email] | [Phone]
Manager | [Manager name]

Period [Start date] - [End date]

Standard Work Week	Hours Worked	Regular Hours	Overtime Hours
40.00	0.00	0.00	0.00

Date(s)	▼ Time In	▼ Lunch Start	▼ Lunch End	▼ Time Out	▼ Hours Worked	▼
[Date]	[Time In]	[Lunch Start]	[Lunch End]	[Time Out]	0.00	
[Date]	[Time In]	[Lunch Start]	[Lunch End]	[Time Out]	0.00	
[Date]	[Time In]	[Lunch Start]	[Lunch End]	[Time Out]	0.00	
[Date]	[Time In]	[Lunch Start]	[Lunch End]	[Time Out]	0.00	
[Date]	[Time In]	[Lunch Start]	[Lunch End]	[Time Out]	0.00	

Involving other people

Do you need to get information from others? One method is to use survey tools and forms. But, don't worry, you can make your own in Excel.

13. Forms

Excel is an excellent tool for designing forms, from basic to complex. You may even create numerous drop-down menus so that users may choose from a pre-defined list of options.

14. Quizzes

Trying to assess someone else's — or even your own — understanding of a topic? You may generate a bank of questions and answers in one worksheet and then have Excel quiz you in another.

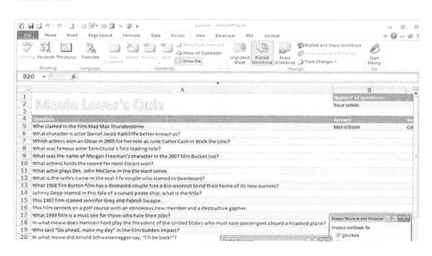

Staying in touch

Relationship management is critical to your career and personal success. Excel, fortunately, makes it simple to stay in contact.

15. CRM

Do you need a simple CRM to remain top of mind with your customers? One may be created in Excel. What's more, the finest part? It will be completely customizable if you build it yourself.

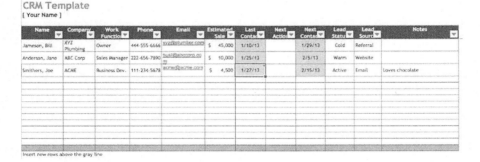

16. Mailing list

Data does not always have to be numerical. Excel is also excellent at handling and categorizing huge lists of names and addresses, making it ideal for your company's holiday party invitation list or the mailing list for a significant promotion or campaign.

You can also mail merge using Excel, which makes printing address labels and other things a lot simpler.

A similar technique may also be used to generate directories, RSVP lists, and other rosters that include a lot of information about individuals.

Just for fun

It doesn't have to be all work and no pleasure when it comes to Excel. You can make a variety of other interesting things using the spreadsheet tool.

17. Historical logs

Whether you want to keep track of the different craft beers you've tried, the exercises you've accomplished, or something else altogether, Excel can help you keep everything organized and logged.

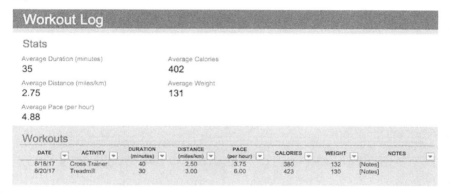

18. Sudoku puzzles

Do you like Sudoku puzzles? You can create your own in Excel, as it turns out, alternatively if you're stuck on a really difficult one.

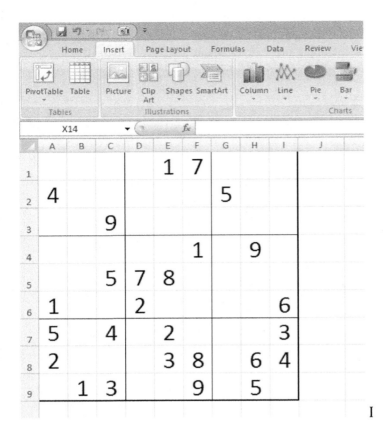

19. Word cloud

Word clouds aren't the most scientific way to portray facts. They are, however, a fascinating (not to mention gorgeous) method to learn about the most often used terms. You guessed it—Excel can be used to make one.

20. Art and animations

Excel's capabilities are going to go well beyond what you may expect. Many individuals have utilized the program to make some very amazing art, ranging from pixelated portraits to animations.

21. Trip planner

Do you have a trip planned? Before you pack your bags and go, make sure you have everything covered by making a handy itinerary. You can even use Excel to create a trip planning template to ensure you don't forget anything (from your budget to flight details!).

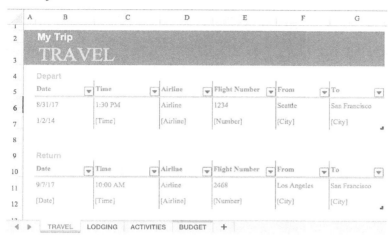

Importance of MS Excel in Our Business and Daily Lives

Formatting Options

Businesses may use a variety of styling options, such as italics, highlighting, and colors, to make the most relevant data stand out from the others. This tool will perform a variety of functions, including whole row highlighting comparing lists and values, to name a few. You may use them to attract attention to specific Accounting entries.

Online Access Availability

Excel is a component of the Office 365 Productivity Suite, which ensures that company owners and staff can view their data across the cloud network without having to worry about file transfers. You may use the same program to view the same file remotely from a web-enabled PC, mobile device, or tablet, making it convenient to make changes if you can't access your PC and need to email the spreadsheet right away.

Organize all of your data in one place

Excel enables you to build spreadsheets larger than 20 A1 documents, with over 1,048,576 rows & 16,384 columns in each spreadsheet, and hundreds of them, or more if your PC is able, in a single file! Via the insert tab, you can easily import from other spreadsheets & add pictures and other items, making it simple to get all of the data you've gathered from different files into one location.

Human Resource Management

While there are other systems for planning this, such as Oracle or QuickBooks, Excel helps you to handle anything in one file! You will quickly find errors when summarising an employee's salaries and salary per hour. This is vital for future control since it allows Human Resource Professionals to take the entire employee journal in bulk and then use it to schedule future credit and determine whether to spend more or not.

Business Analysis

Business analysis is the most common usage of Microsoft Excel in the workplace.

Business analysis is the process of utilizing data to help people make better decisions. Businesses naturally collect data in everyday operations, such as website traffic, supply expenditure, product sales, insurance claims, and so on.

People Management

You might be shocked to find that 1 of the most common use of Excel in the workplaces to manage people.

Microsoft Excel is a fantastic tool for organizing data on individuals, whether they're workers, clients, supporters, or attendance at training sessions.

Personal information may be conveniently saved and accessed using Excel. An individual record may be stored in a spreadsheet column or row with information such as email address, name, employee starting date, things bought last contact and subscription status.

Managing the Operations

Many organizations rely significantly on Excel to run their everyday operations. When it comes to business, logistics may be rather tricky. Inventory flows must be managed to keep operations operating smoothly – and to avoid overstocking on certain goods. This includes keeping track of the supplier and customer transactions, putting together a calendar of important events, and managing time & schedules.

Performance Reporting

Performance monitoring & reporting is the sort of business analysis that may be accomplished using Microsoft Excel. Many accountants, for example, continue to use Excel (in part because it is compatible with accounting cloud-based software). A pivot table is a standard approach to transform data into performance reports in Excel. You may easily extract relevant information from a dataset by introducing a pivot table & attaching it to the data. Pivot tables come with a number of built-in functions that enable you to do activities like counting & summing certain sorts of data inside a data set.

Office Administration

Much of the data required for accounting & financial reporting, also business analysis & performance reporting, is entered and stored in Excel by office administrators. Excel is important in office administrations for assisting everyday duties like invoicing, contacting suppliers & customers and paying bills, in addition to recordkeeping. It's a multi-functional program for tracking and organizing workplace operations.

Strategic Analysis

Strategic analysis is a kind of Excel analysis in which business choices are strongly linked to data and formulae on a spreadsheet. You use Excel to help you make decisions about investments & asset allocations.

Project Management

Despite the fact that Project staff have access to the project administration software that was designed specifically for them, Excel Workbooks' often a viable option.

Projects are a kind of commercial activity that has a budget & a start and finish date. Project plans may be entered into the workbook that can subsequently be utilized to monitor progress and stay on track. One benefit of utilizing Excel's that you could simply share project worksheets with others, even if they are not familiar with or don't have access to proprietary software.

Managing Programs

Excel is an excellent program management tool. It may be customized to handle the unique features of particular software. Because Microsoft Excel's widely used, program records may be readily handled by various persons and passed over to a new manager when the time comes.

The program is similar to a project, except it may be continuous and reliant on user engagement. Managers may use MS Excel to allocate resources, monitor progress, and keep track of participant information.

Contract Administration

MS Excel is popular among contract administrators because it makes it simple to keep track of contract specifics such as milestones, payments, dates, and deliverables.

There are several contract management templates to choose from, each of which may be customized to fit the contract stage or type of contract lifecycles.

Account Management

Because they receive and must keep client data, an account manager is often expected to be proficient Excel users. An account manager's role is to maintain ties with the company's current customers. Customer loyalty & repeat sales are important objectives. It's a marketing-oriented position that's a popular choice among MBA grads. Excel is often used in account management ever since it makes sharing and maintaining customer files straightforward.

Chapter 2: Microsoft Excel 2022

Brief Review 0f Previous Versions of Excel

In 1985, the spreadsheet application was released solely for Macintosh, with a Microsoft version coming in 1987. A brief introduction about versions of MS excel except for the latest one (which we will discuss late in this chapter) below summarizes all of the many aspects of different versions of Excel, beginning with the first version in 1985 and ending with the most recent version in 2022. So here we are, with the release of the many versions of Microsoft Excel for Windows, which you may come across.

Version 1: Released in 1985. This version of Excel was initially offered solely for Macintosh computers. Many Excel users are unaware of this, and it may seem weird. Microsoft had previously attempted to produce a spreadsheet application called Multiplan in 1982, but it was unsuccessful. Until 2016, Excel versions for various operating systems were known by distinct names.

Excel 2: Released in 1987. To correlate to the Mac version, the initial MS Excel edition for Windows was designated "2." It was a port of the Mac "Excel 2" and contained a run-time version for Windows.

Excel 3: Released in 1990. Toolbars, outlining, drawing capabilities, 3D charts, add-in support, and many more additional innovations and features were included in this next edition.

Excel 4: Released in 1992. Version 4 was the first "famous" version of Excel. Many usability enhancements were implemented, including AutoFill, which was originally offered in this version.

Excel 5: Released in 1993. Excel 5 was a significant update. It had multi-worksheet workbooks as well as Macros AND VBA support. Excel became more susceptible to macro virus assaults as a result of these new features, which REMAINED to be a concern until the 2007 edition.

Excel 95: Released in 1995. It was the first main 32-bit version of Excel, and it was known as Excel 95. Excel 5 featured a 32-bit version as well, although it was not extensively utilized owing to distribution issues. Excel 95 is pretty comparable to Excel 5 in terms of features. You might also be asking why Excel 6 isn't available. Beginning with Excel 7, all MS Office apps have been using the same version number, so the version numbering has been modified.

Excel 97: Released in 1997. This version included a new VBA developer interface, data validation, User Forms, and much more. Do you remember Clippy, the obnoxious Office Assistant? He was also a member of this version.

Excel 2000: Released in 1999. HTML as a local file format, a "self-repair" capability, an upgraded clipboard, modeless user forms and pivot charts are among the new features.

Excel 2002: Released in 2001. This was the first time Excel was included in Office XP. The vast list of new features didn't contribute much to the ordinary user's experience. The new capability that enabled you to restore your work if Excel crashes were among the most important innovations. This version also had a helpful feature called product activation technology (commonly called copy protection), which limits the usage of the program to one computer at a time. Before determining whether or not to update, you had to think about the consequences.

Microsoft Office Excel 2003: Released in 2003. Improved XML support, a new "list range" tool, Smart Tag upgrades, and updated statistical functions were among the new features in this version. The majority of consumers did not consider the data upgrade beneficial.

Microsoft Office Excel 2007: Released in 2007. Excel underwent significant modifications in this Windows edition. The Ribbon interface was introduced, as well as a change in the file format type from .xls to the now-familiar .xlsx and .xlsm. This modification improved Excel's security (referred to the difficulties with macro viruses in previous versions) and allowed for additional row data storage (over one million). The charting features have also been considerably enhanced.

Microsoft Office Excel 2010: Released in 2010. Sparkline graphics, an updated Solver, pivot table slicers, and a 64-bit version were among the new additional features in this MS Excel version.

Microsoft Excel 2013: Released in 2013. Over 50 new functions were included in this edition, as well as a single-document interface suggested pivot tables and charts and additional charting improvements.

Microsoft Excel 2016: Released in 2016. Despite the fact that they were separate versions of the program, Excel for Windows and Mac was known as the same thing after this version came out. If you had a subscription to Office 365, you get unique Excel Internet updates that may drastically improve your user experience. Older versions and those purchased from a store are consequently at a disadvantage. Histograms (to illustrate the frequency in data), Power Pivot (which allowed for the input of greater levels of data and included its own language), and Pareto charts (to display data trends) were some of the new features in this edition.

Microsoft Excel 2019: Released in 2019. This version had all of the capabilities found in previous versions of Excel, as well as some new ones. The new charts, which provide a unique twist to data presentation, are one of the most noticeable new additions. Funnel charts and Map charts are two examples of modern data presentation charts that make your data seem tidy; they both were added in this version. In addition, the option of using 3D images in your workbooks was introduced.

If you have an older version of MS Excel, it will probably work with newer files if you use the compatibility mode. Keep in mind that previous versions have many fewer features that are understandable if you've been paying attention to the changing features in the previous versions. Some of them may not be functional with the newer operating systems, but it's a good idea to try out several versions and look at how the same file appears in each.

All about MS Excel 2022

Microsoft Excel 2022 updates were launched on May 11, 2022. These updates will enable you to enjoy a seamless experience with all the features of the software. If you already have Excel installed on your device, you should carry out these updates to help you in maximizing the potential of the app.

Microsoft Excel 2022 will have an improved interface, new tools that will enable users to manage data in Microsoft Excel more flexibly, and other enhancements, according to Microsoft. In Excel 2022, two brand new features will be included. The first, known as dynamic arrays, will add to Excel's data-analytics property. The spreadsheet editor comes with a huge number of pre-made formulas that may be used to do things like calculating the average quarterly income for the last two years. In most cases, a formula's output is condensed into one spreadsheet cell, which might cause formatting challenges for advanced business calculations with several outputs. To save time, dynamic arrays arrange findings into different cells automatically.

Excel will also get a feature called XLOOKUP from Microsoft, which allows users to look for data in a particular spreadsheet row rather than wading through the whole spreadsheet. This is especially beneficial in complicated documents with a big number of identical components. A user may, for example, find the row having the name of a vehicle component and then utilize the XLOOKUP option to rapidly move to the cell in that same row showing the component's price.

Detailed Feature Updates

Excel has made its users happy and contended by introducing all the latest and most useful tools and features in its software. In the upcoming latest version of Excel 2022, there are some significant feature updates that people who frequently use excel would love to read about. If you want to know about all the new features, then keep going further in this chapter. All the feature updates that will be included in the brand new version of Excel is Excel 2022, are discussed below.

Automatically Use New Data Types: Excel suggests converting a data value that matches a geographic location or a stock to the appropriate associated data type of Stocks or Geography when you input it.

Excel Data Types:

Stocks and Geography: Excel may be used to get geographic and stock data. It's as simple as typing any text into a cell then turning it into the Geography data or Stocks data type. As they have a link to an online web data source, these 2 data types are termed linked data types. This link enables you to get rich, intriguing data that you may work with and update.

Note: If Excel recognizes what you're typing as a geographic location or tradable financial instrument, it will suggest a linked data type for you to use (Stocks or Geography). Only Microsoft 365 customers or those having a free Microsoft Account may access the Geography or Stocks data types.

Linked data types: It provides you with real-world facts. New linked data types in Excel deliver you data and facts on hundreds of topics to help you achieve your objectives.

Creating Data Types: You may use the Advanced Dialog to manually pick the columns that make up the Data Type you're making.

Unhide Many Sheets at the Same Time: It's no longer necessary to unhide a single sheet at a time; instead, you may unhide numerous concealed sheets at the same time. To make a worksheet invisible, you may hide it. Although the data in hidden worksheets is hidden, it may still be accessed from other workbooks or worksheets, and hidden worksheets can be readily unhidden as required. To un-hide sheets, right-click any visible sheet or the sheet tab you wish to hide. Choose one of the following options from the menu that appears:

Select Hide to conceal the sheet.

To reveal hidden sheets, pick them in Unhide dialogue box that opens, then click OK.

To choose numerous sheets, perform one of the following:

Hold CTRL while clicking the items to choose them.

Press and then hold SHIFT, then change your selection using the up or down arrow keys.

Integrated Stock Prices: With their new Data Types capability, Microsoft stated that Excel users would be able to extract real-time stock price data right into their spreadsheet cells. When predicting anything, particularly stocks, having access to previous data is essential. We can design (and share) our own algorithms that automatically examine thousands of stocks and indicate those we may wish to invest in using this data accessible to Excel users. Although such data is currently accessible via third parties, obtaining it for free and without needing to input files on a regular basis would be a significant victory for personal financial enthusiasts.

Stock Name	52 Wk Low	52 Wk High	Price	% Change
🏛 Microsoft Corp (XNAS:MSFT)	$93.96	$158.67	$158.67	+0.82%
🏛 Alphabet Inc (XNAS:GOOG)	$983.00	$1,365.00	$1,360.40	+1.25%
🏛 Verizon Communications Inc (XNYS:VZ)	$52.28	$62.22	$61.29	+0.02%
🏛 Walt Disney Co (XNYS:DIS)	$100.38	$153.41	$145.70	+0.28%
🏛 Apple Inc (XNAS:AAPL)	$142.00	$289.91	$289.91	+1.98%
🏛 Facebook Inc (XNAS:FB)	$125.89	$208.66	$207.79	+1.30%

Automate Data Analysis with Excel's Ideas Feature: Ideas is an artificial intelligence feature in Excel 2022 that is accessible with Office 365 subscriptions. Excel can swiftly evaluate your data with Ideas and give you insights you may not have spotted otherwise. Now, I don't think this technology will ever replace financial analysts (there's a reason it's named "Ideas" rather than "Answers"), but you should see it as a way to get a second opinion on our data or to automate the analysis-creation process. It will be fascinating to observe how this technology evolves in the next years, as well as how often Excel users will utilize it.

Ideas might be beneficial in the following scenarios, for example:

Rank data and find objects that are considerably smaller or bigger as compared to the rest of the population by analyzing transactions;

Using trend analysis to identify patterns in data that have developed over time;

Identifying major anomalies in data points, such as fraudulent transactions or possibly erroneous

Drawing attention to instances where a single element accounts for a major amount of the entire value.

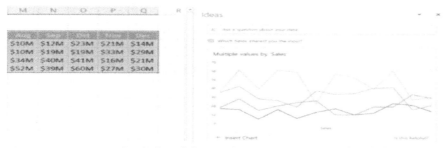

You may access the 'Ideas' from the main Home tab of the Ribbon if you have an Office 365 subscription. However, in order to utilize this functionality, you should have an internet connection.

Simpler Conditional Formulas with IFS, MAXIFS, and MINIFS: You can write formulas that include numerous tests more easily than before using IFS, MAXIFS, and MINIFS. Many Excel users used to "nest" many 'IF' functions in the same calculation before IFS became available. When you needed to do a computation based on one or more circumstances, this was a frequent approach. However, with the development of IFS, such formulations have been substantially simplified. For example, observe how just a single IFS function is needed in the formula written below to run three tests on the data in cell A2. This method avoids the need for several IF functions, which would have been necessary previously. MAXIFS and MINIFS, like IFS, allow you to run many tests on your data. When utilizing MAXIFS, when all of the tests are passed, Excel will give the highest value. When utilizing MINIFS, on the other hand, when all of the conditions are passed, Excel returns the lowest number. Excel 2022 users will have access to these capabilities. They're also accessible to Office 365 subscribers who have access to Excel.

XLOOKUP – A Better and Easier Alternative to VLOOKUP: Beginning in February 2020, Microsoft will bring XLOOKUP to Excel as part of Office 365. VLOOKUP and comparable functions like HLOOKUP and INDEX are pale in comparison to XLOOKUP. While Excel will retain these older functionalities, many people are going to discover XLOOKUP to be much more easy and intuitive. Most people will discover that XLOOKUP is significantly more powerful.

The following are some of the key distinctions between other lookup functions and XLOOKUP:

XLOOKUP uses an exact match by default, while VLOOKUP and HLOOKUP use an approximate match.

Unlike VLOOKUP and HLOOKUP, you do not need to provide a row index number or a column index number with XLOOKUP.

With XLOOKUP, the order of rows and columns is unimportant. This is because, when used as a replacement for VLOOKUP, it can look left or right. When used as a replacement for HLOOKUP, it can also look above or below.

XLOOKUP eliminates the need for an IFERROR function by allowing you to describe what happened if your search value isn't found.

	A	B	C	D	E	F	G	H
							=XLOOKUP(H2,B3:B15,D3:D15,"Item Not Found")	
1								
2		Item	Description	Unit Price	QOH		Part Number	C003
3		C001	Creme, Aloe Vera Hand, 9 oz	6.99	143		Unit Price	12.99
4		C002	Creme, Extra Moisturizing Hand, 9 oz	7.49	109		Quantity On Hand	72
5		C003	Creme, Hand and Body, 16 oz	12.99	72			
6		L001	Lotion, Organic Body, 9 oz	7.99	68			
7		L002	Lotion, Organic Body, 16 oz	14.99	148			
8		L003	Lotion, Organic Body, 24 oz	21.99	106			
9		L201	Lotion, Extra Moisturizing Body, 9 oz	6.99	165			
10		L202	Lotion, Organic Hand and Body, 9 oz	8.49	138			
11		L203	Lotion, Organic Hand and Body, 16 oz	15.99	63			
12		M101	Mask, Organic Facial, 9 oz	13.99	89			
13		M102	Mask, Wrinkle Reducing Facial, 9 oz	18.99	34			
14		M201	Mask, Wrinkle Reducing Facial, 16 oz	35.99	58			
15		M202	Mask, Wrinkle Reducing Facial, 24 oz	53.99	69			

VLOOKUP, IFERROR, HLOOKUP and INDEX/MATCH are all combined into one simplified Excel function with XLOOKUP. This is the feature that you will all be teaching your children how to use before their first job interview, and it is one that you will assure to use on a regular basis within the corporate sector.

Dynamic Arrays: Another new feature update that is now only accessible with a subscription to Office 365 is dynamic arrays. You can use dynamic arrays to create one single formula that affects numerous cells at the same time without having to replicate the formula to all of them. You also don't need to utilize the CTRL + SHIFT + ENTER keyboard sequence to enter a typical array formula if you're using an Excel version that supports dynamic arrays. Furthermore, if you're using an Excel version that has dynamic arrays function, you'll have access to six additional functions to help you take use of this newfound ability. FILTER, RANDARRY, SORT, SEQUENCE, UNIQUE and SORTBY are the six functions.

Illustrating Dynamic Arrays: Let's see how to use the new FILTER function to provide a basic example of dynamic arrays. The FILTER function, as its name suggests, may be used to filter data in a range or table using a formula. The syntax is straightforward, as demonstrated below.

=FILTER (array (range or table), include (a Boolean array for which items to include))

The basic FILTER example presented should demonstrate the value of dynamic arrays: they let you evaluate data using formulas, and the formula outputs are related to the raw data set but do not disrupt it. As a result, instead of copying the data numerous times, you may do several sorts of analyses on the very same underlying data set. Do you recall wanting to create a complicated formula, looking for it on the web, and then copying and pasting it into your worksheet with the instructions to type ctrl+shift+enter after that? Who wonders why you had to do that, but it worked like a charm! That formula you came upon was the formula of an Array. Curly brackets around these formulas (auto-inserted with ctrl+shift+enter) were required to notify Excel what to assume since they produce various responses.

Microsoft unveiled a new set of functions in early 2019 that has radically changed the way we create complicated calculations as users. These new Dynamic Array functions have reduced the complex/lengthy formulas of the past into easy, dynamic functions that everyone can use.....and the greatest thing is that you no longer need to utilize the ctrl+shift+enter keyboard sequence! UNIQUE was one of the initial capabilities included in Microsoft's initial suite. Simply give unique a range of cells, and it will return each and every one of the unique values it discovers in individual cells (eliminating duplicate values). Even further, if your set of values expands or contracts over time, the list provided by the UNIQUE formula will update accordingly.

H3					f_x		=UNIQUE($D$4:$D$11)	

	A	B	C	D	E	F	G	H
1								
2								
3				State			Unique States:	Ohio
4				Ohio				California
5				California				New York
6				New York				New Mexico
7				Ohio				Florida
8				Ohio				
9				New Mexico				
10				Florida				
11				Florida				
12								

The Dark Mode Addition which make Things Simpler

Dark mode users claim that it improves the clarity between the text you're reading and the surrounding environment. This should potentially make computer reading simpler. Medium grey and Black are the default themes of Microsoft Office. By choosing a dark theme, you may alter the look of Office products like Microsoft Word, Excel, PowerPoint and Outlook. The dark option would be much better, making everything considerably darker and easier on the eyes. The dark backdrop may make late-night editing and writing much easier. Microsoft Word's dark option currently just darkens the document's borders, leaving the remainder bright white. You will be capable to darken the whole paper in a future release.

Overall Benefits of Using MS Excel 2022

MS Excel is extensively used for a variety of reasons, including the ease with which data can be information can be inserted and withdrawn and saved with no effort. A few fundamental and essential advantages of using Microsoft Excel 2022 are listed below:

41

Easy To Recover Data: Finding information written on a paper might take longer, but that isn't the situation with excel spreadsheets. It's simple to locate and retrieve data.

Mathematical Formulas application: With the formulas feature in MS Excel, doing mathematical calculations has become simpler and less time-consuming.

Easy To Save Data: MS Excel is extensively used to save and analyses data since there is no restriction to the quantity of data that can be recorded in a spreadsheet. Filtering data in Excel is simple and straightforward.

More Secure: These spreadsheets are password protected on a laptop or desktop computer, and the risk of losing them is far lower than data stored in registers or on paper.

Clearer and *Neater and Visibility of data:* Analyzing data gets simpler when it is recorded in tabular form. As a result, information is more understandable and readable in a spreadsheet.

All Data at One Place: When the documentation was completed, data was previously held in various files and registers. More than one worksheet may now be added to a single MS Excel file, making this more practical.

Excel allows users to analyze, organize, and evaluate quantitative results, enabling senior staff and managers to make key choices that might affect the firm with the knowledge they need. Employees that are taught in advanced Excel functions will be able to present their data more effectively to senior management. It's also a necessary talent for individuals who want to work their way to the top. Employers and Employees can benefit from superior

Excel knowledge. Let's take a closer look at the benefits of Excel when it is a part of the company's regular staff training.

Advantages of Excel 2022 for Employees

Advanced Excel training may help your employees in a variety of ways, from improving their value to learning new tools to boost their job performance.

Sharpening Your Skill Set: To progress in your profession, you must continue to study and polish your skills. Appropriate training of Excel focuses on a variety of important abilities that may be used and appreciated in practically every job role. You should be able to:

Visualize, modify, and analyses data after training.

Develop equations that will enable you to deliver additional information on critical corporate activities, including workflow, financial estimates, project efficiency, and inventory levels and utilization as well as budgets,

Create an easy-to-understand data collection that higher management may utilize to assess current initiatives or conditions in the firm.

Create spreadsheets that better organize data and provide a clearer view of what's being entered.

Read and understand data and spreadsheets from other departments, suppliers, and customers.

The ability to evaluate data at a higher level allows you to provide solutions to business challenges.

Organize, balance, and maintain complicated inventory and financial accounts.

Set up tracking systems for various departments and activities, as well as distinct workflow processes.

Comprehensive MS Excel training will supply organizations with higher-skilled personnel as well as tools to assist workers in operating more efficiently in their existing roles and preparing them for advancement to higher-level roles.

Improving Your Productivity and Efficiency: When dealing with big volumes of data and computations, Excel is a critical tool for increasing productivity and helping employees to be more efficient. When you have a deeper understanding of Excel, you will be able to utilize its more complex capabilities, which will help you to finish jobs and analyses data more rapidly.

Making You Better at Organizing Data: Spreadsheets are a popular tool for gathering and organizing data. MS Excel is in its most basic form. It enables you to meticulously arrange all of the data while also allowing you to arrange the information in whatever manner you like. Data in its raw form may be overwhelming and difficult to understand. With Excel's amazing features, you'll be able to better organize your data, do computations as needed, and sort the data so that it can be properly examined and transferred to charts or graphs for easier viewing.

It Can Make Your Job Easier: The more familiar you are with Excel, the faster you will be able to manage the system. Microsoft Excel has a number of shortcuts that may help you work quicker and even discover more complex Excel tactics that you may use throughout the full Microsoft Office suite. You'll also be able to utilize the information in your Excel spreadsheet in a number of tools, decreasing the need to re-enter data and improving the efficiency of your workflow. The simpler your job is to do, the more prepared you are to do it and more probably you are to love it.

Advantages of Advanced Excel for Employers

Advanced Excel knowledge and expertise may bring several advantages for both your staff and your company.

It boosts your company's productivity by increasing efficiency.

It enables you to increase employee understanding with little cost and effort.

It relieves your IT support team of stress, allowing them to concentrate on more productive activities like system updates, security maintenance, and hardware installation and maintenance.

MS Excel 2022 Tips and Tricks

There are numerous ideas and tricks which can make things easier, and you can use any of them to make a difficult situation seem easy. A few of them are mentioned below.

Convert rows to columns

By selecting the cells, you would like to turn around, going to Edit, Copy, choosing a new cell, and then moving to Edit, Paste Special, you can transform columns to row and vice versa. Finally, press OK after ticking the Transpose button on the dialogue box.

Calculate time

Put the formula =A2-A1 in a cell, where the earlier date and A2 are later. Remember to convert the reference cell to numeric form by highlighting it, going to Format, Cells…, choosing the Number column, and clicking Number from the Category list.

Enter "URL" as text

Add an apostrophe at the URL start, such as www.futureplan.com, to discourage Excel from turning written Web sites into hyperlinks.

Calculate cumulative Sum

Column A should contain the number to be inserted, such as A1 to A5, and column B should contain the formula =SUM ($A$1: A1). Go to Edit, Filled, Down and choose the cells beside ones with a number (in our case, B1 to B5). The cumulative sum of the numbers in columns A1 through A5 is placed in the adjacent section.

Remove hyperlinks

Suppose Excel already has converted the written URL to a hyperlink. In that case, you will undo it just by right-clicking on the offensive address and clicking Hyperlink, Delete Hyperlink from the pop-up menu.

Fit tables to the page

Click File, Page Configuration, select the Page section, click the Match to radio icon, and choose 1 page wide to allow the tables exactly to fit on the page. Click Delete on the tall box, which will now be clean.

Hide the Data

Highlight the appropriate cell and choose Format, Cells… to mask some confidential data from view. To render the data available again, go to the Numbers tab, pick Custom from Category: Chart, click doubled on the Type, input box, and enter, then undo the procedure.

Make Use of the template

When you're creating a fresh worksheet, templates will save you a lot of time. Click the workbook Solutions tab from the File menu, then select a design from the Chart.

Lotus users' Assistant

If you've switched from Lotus 1 to 2 to 3 and are having trouble with Excel, you can get assistance tailored to your circumstance by supporting Lotus 1 to 2 to 3 Help.

Formula browser

Select a cell and use "Paste" on the main toolbar to paste the formula. Select the required feature from the list box. Now press OK after clicking the cells in which one you like the target to execute the action.

Autofill

If you always use the same list of separate worksheets, you might consider adding it to the AutoFill list; this can save you a lot of time in the future. Click the Custom List tab from the Tools, Options... menu after selecting the set. Select Import, then Well.

Auto Calculator

If you don't want to type in a feature to measure a number dependent on a row or column of numbers, just pick the numbers and look at the status bar; you'll see the sum of the chosen cells there. Furthermore, when you right-click on sum, a pop-up menu with additional simple calculation functions will appear.

Enter the time

Click a cell and write =today () to enter the present day or period () or write =now (). Anytime you start the sheet, Excel updates the outcome, so it's all up to date.

Enter a fixed time

Click a cell and click Ctrl +; for date and Ctrl +: for the period if you want Excel to insert the latest time or date and adjust it at the point. E.g., to display the last day the sheet was updated.

Currently active cell

If you miss your location when browsing through your spreadsheet, click the CTRL Backspace keys to return to the actual active cell.

See the bigger image

You might like to move to Full display mode if you're operating on a big sheet: clicking on View, Full Display. To switch to a regular browser, click it again.

Automatically Fit the text

Find the correct column and click Format>>column>>AutoFit Selection to make your job appear neater.

Fast copy

It's fast to repeat the equation or figure inside the cells above the one you're in by pressing Ctrl + '.

Easy and Fast multiple Entry

Choose the target cells, type the formula as normal, and click Ctrl + Enter if you need to type a formula in multiple cells at once.

Auto Selection

By keeping down Ctrl when clicking on the individual cells, you may pick unconnected cells.

Hide comments

Using the insert Comment feature, you may hide details and other comments. Select a cell, then press Insert, Comment, and then enter your text. When you're finished, click outside from the input box. When you move your cursor over the appropriate cell, the statement may show.

Re-coloring the lines

By going to Tools, Options, View, selecting the Color, List box, and picking a new color from the palette, you can adjust the color of the grid. Choosing white essentially eliminates the grid.

Angle your entry

Select the toolbar with the help of right-clicking, choose Chart, and choose one of the "ab" icons on the current toolbar to render Excel display text in the cell at a 45-degree angle. Change the text to whatever angle you like; if you want customized angles, click on the cells & choose Layout Cell from the pop-up screen, then choose the Alignment tab, click on the Text marker in the Orientation pane move the Text pointer.

Zoom in

By highlighting the appropriate cells, selecting the arrows on the Zoom button on the toolbar, and choosing Selection from the chart, you can make Excel showing just the field you're working in.

Another standard entry path

When you click [Return] while editing cells, the mouse goes away. Click Tools, Options..., and then Edit to adjust the course. After entering the list box, click the Move selection button and choose another course from the drop-down menu.

Set decimal points

Click the Edit tab from the Tools, Choice, and Edit tab menus. To fix the numbers of decimal points, position a click in the Set decimal checkbox and then use the arrow in the Places.

Sort the columns quickly

Selecting a column and clicking the Sort Increasing or Sort Decreasing buttons is the easiest way to sort it into a hierarchy

Typing while Erasing entries

If you type the formula incorrectly, click Esc to clear the contents of the cell.

See Formulas

Through going to Tools, Options..., choosing the Display tab, and ticking the Formulas check button, you can see all of the formulas at once.

Switch off 0s.

By choosing Tools, Options..., the Display tab, or unticking the 0-values tick box, you will prevent 0s from filling up your sheets.

Customize the dates

The Customized cell format allows you to change the layout of a period in a cell. To do so, type a date in such a cell, select Format, Cells, Standard in the Category, window, Type, input box, and M repeatedly until the correct format appears in the Sample field.

Column Copy Quickly

By clicking doubled on a cell's handle, you might fill out cells in such a column. Excel can duplicate the tapped cell in any of the cells below it, stopping until it approaches a cell without blanks on both sides.

Merge cell contents

Click on cell C1 and type =A1&B1 to combine the data of cells B1 and A1. Since the product is a text string rather than a sum, combining 10 and 7 yields 107 rather than 17.

	A	B	C
1	10	7	107
2			

Dynamic formatting

Excel may be configured to warn you of important figures in the cell by changing the text's size and color when a certain requirement is met. Select a cell (for example, the cell containing your bank balance total) and choose Type, Conditional formatting... In the pop-up dialogue, choose the conditions (E.g., "Cell value < 0") and press the Format... icon. Now, in the Color list box, choose a new color and press OK. To end, click OK once more.

Whenever your chosen figure goes below zero, Excel can now represent it in the new color.

Cell's Border connector

By selecting a group of similar cells and clicking Format Cells, choosing the Border section and clicking the Outline icon, you may create a border around them – for example, all the totals.

Entries should be shrunk to fit their cells.

Using Shrink to Suit choice in Excel, you will compel Spreadsheets to access the entire text. Select Format, Cells>>Alignment tab >> check the Shrink to Matchbox. The more texts you get, the smaller the cell would be, but this isn't realistic for tiny cells with a ton of material.

Create hyperlinks

Enter a name for the connection in a cell and press Ctrl + K to position connections in cells that allow you to launch other documents with a single click. Select File... from the drop-down menu. Go to the file you want to connect to and choose it. Double-click it and then choose OK. Excel can now switch to the file anytime you select in that cell.

Chapter 3: Microsoft Excel 2022 Basics

How to open Microsoft Excel?

Excel can be run in the same way as any other Windows application. If you're using a graphical user interface (GUI), such as Windows XP, Vista, or 7, follow the measures below:

Go to the Start menu.

Choose all programs.

Take your cursor to Microsoft Excel.

Click on Microsoft Excel.

Understanding the Ribbon

In Excel, the Ribbon gives shortcuts to different commands. An action taken by the user is a command. Printing a document, creating a new document, and so on are examples of commands.

Ribbon Start Button

The ribbon start button is used to execute commands such as generating new records, printing, saving existing writing, and having access to Excel's customization options, among others.

Ribbon tabs

These are used for group commands that are alike. Basic commands like editing data to render it more presentable, searching, and locating unique

data inside the spreadsheet are performed on the home page.

Ribbon bar

These bars are used to group commands that are identical. For example, to organize all of the actions that are applied for aligning data together is used.

Understanding the Worksheet

A worksheet is a collection of columns and rows. A cell is formed when a column and a row intersect. Data is recorded in cells. A cell address is used to identify each cell individually. Letters are used to mark columns, and numbers are used to label rows.

A list of worksheets is referred to as a workbook. A workbook in Excel comprises three sheets to begin with. To meet your needs, you can erase or add more sheets. Sheet1, Sheet2, and so on are the default names for the spreadsheets. You should rename them to something more important, like Daily Expenses or Monthly Budget.

Windows Components for Microsoft Excel

It's important to know where everything is in the window when you start using Microsoft Excel. So, ahead, are all the big components that you should be aware of before diving into the realm of Microsoft Excel.

A cell that is selected is known as an active cell. A rectangular box will be used to illustrate it, and its whereabouts will be displayed in the address bar. Clicking on a cell or using your arrow keys can activate it. You can double-click on a cell or use F2 to edit it.

A column is a vertical grouping of cells. A single worksheet may have up to 16384 columns. From A to XFD, each column will have a unique letter for identification. By clicking on a column's header, you can select it.

A row is a horizontal grouping of cells. A single worksheet may have up to 1048576 rows. For identification, each row has a unique number ranging from 1 to 1048576. By pressing the row number on the left side of the browser, you can select it.

Fill Handle

This is a tiny dot in the active cell's lower right corner. It helps you with inserting numeric values, text sequences, ranges, and serial numbers, among other things. The Address Bar displays the active cell's address. If you pick more than one cell, the first cell's address in the range will be shown. Below the Ribbon is the formula bar, which is an input bar. It displays the contents of the selected cell and allows you to type a formula into a cell.

The name of your workbook would appear in the title bar, accompanied by the program name ("Microsoft Excel"). The file menu, like many other programs, is a plain menu. It has choices such as Open, Save, Print, Save As, Excel Options, New, Share.

Quick Access Toolbar

A toolbar that allows you to easily analyze the actions you use the most. By clicking new options to the "quick access toolbar," you can add your favorite options.

Ribbon Tab

Beginning with Microsoft Excel 2007, all choice menus have been replaced by ribbons. Ribbon tabs are a set of various command groups that include additional options.

Worksheet Column

This tab displays all the worksheets in the workbook. Sheet1, Sheet2, and Sheet3 are the names of the three worksheets that will appear in your latest workbook, respectively.

Status Bar

At the base of the Excel pane, there is a thin bar. When you begin using Excel, it will be of immediate assistance.

You will build a toolbar in Excel that contains the commands you need the most. The Easy Access Toolbar helps you to quickly and efficiently complete your most common tasks.

1. Choose the File tab from the top left corner of your browser.

2. Choose Excel Options from the dropdown menu. This will bring up the Excel Options dialogue window.

3. Choose Customize from the left sidebar. The customization choices for your Quick Access Toolbar will appear.

To add a function to your toolbar, follow the steps below:

1. Choose a command from the left-hand scrolling menu.

2. Choose Include. The command has now been added to the right-hand list. The up or down arrows on the side of the browser may be used to reorder the commands on the toolbar.

3. Under the Ribbon box, choose Show Quick Access Toolbar.

4. Choose OK. The Quick Access Toolbar will now show below the Ribbon.

How to Extend Columns and Rows of a Cell

When you start making use of excel application, you will find out that at a point, the words you type in a cell cut into the column of another cell. Here I want to address how to resolve this issue. I will guide you on how to adjust both columns and rows.

First, let me address how to extend the column of a cell. To extend the column of your cell, take these steps:

Click the column heading you want to extend, example column A.

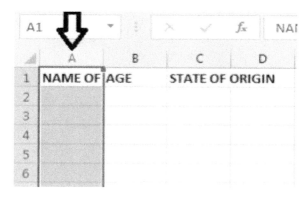

About to extend column A

Position your cursor over the line in the column heading, press down the left button of your mouse and drag to the right.

Also, to extend any row in your spreadsheet, take these steps:

Click the row heading you want to extend, example row 2.

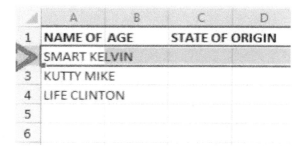

About to extend row 2

Position your cursor over the line in the row heading, hold down the left button of your mouse and drag up or down.

A Cell If you have gone through Biology class before now, you must have heard about cell as that is one of the major topics you were taught. In that Biology study, we found out that a cell is a basic and building unit of life. The same applies when it comes to excel spreadsheet program.

In excel study, a cell is the basic unit that builds the spreadsheet program where data is entered. Cells are the building blocks that form excel. Without cells, there is no excel. It is the intersections of columns and row lines that form cells.

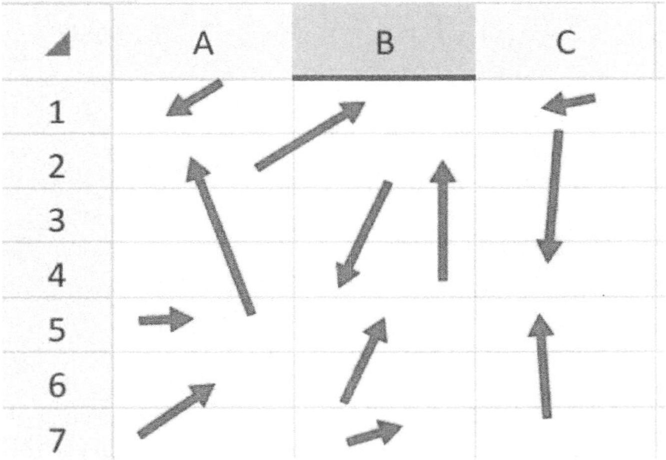

The cells of excel spreadsheet From the above picture, the rectangular boxes where the head arrows point at are know as cells. They are the building blocks of excel application.

A Spreadsheet The term spreadsheet means a working environment of excel program. Using an exercise book as a reference point, a spreadsheet is like a leave (a page) of an exercise book. It is just a document containing rows and columns where data are entered. A spreadsheet can simply be referred to as just sheet.

Workbook A workbook can simply be referred to as combination of many spreadsheets. Going with the illustration I made in spreadsheet term, a workbook takes the position of an exercise book. If you want to prepare data containing expenses you made from year 2000 to year 2020, you can do that in a work with each spreadsheet having the financial report of each year. With time, I will guide you on how to create many spreadsheets in one excel file to form a workbook.

Cursor A cursor is defined as a movable indicator on a computer screen which is meant to affect any spot or command of excel. In this teaching, when I instruct you to drag your cursor to a particular part of excel environment, it implies you should take the pointer to that spot.

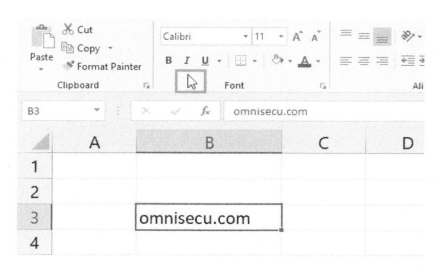

Cursor at a spot of excel screen (pointing Italics command)

Entering Data in Excel

Selecting/Highlighting Cell and Cells

Let me chip in something at this point, when I instruct you should select a cell, what I want you to do is to just click the cell once. This makes the cell to be selected.

If I say you should select or highlight cells, what you are to do is to take your cursor to the cell where you want to start highlighting. Make sure the cross-like sign shows, then press down the left button of your mouse and drag to the direction of the cells you want to select. Once you get to the last cell, release your finger from the left button of your mouse because the cells are selected/highlighted at that point.

How to Edit Data in a Cell

If you want to edit the data you already typed in a cell, double-click the cell containing the data, and then start making the changes you want. When you are done, just click out (I mean you should click a different cell or any other part of the spreadsheet environment).

How to Copy Text in a Cell

You can easily copy the text in excel cells. To complete this task, double-click inside the cell, highlight the text and right-click and then select *copy* option. Also, you can just click the cell containing the text and then press *Ctrl + C* on your computer's keyboard to copy the text.

How to Create More Spreadsheets to Build a Workbook

If you want to create more spreadsheets that will form a workbook, take this my guide:

As you opened an excel blank page, take your cursor to the button part of the spreadsheet.

Click the enclosed + icon at the button and a new spreadsheet is added.

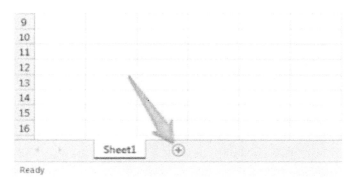

Click the + icon to add a new spreadsheet Take the above steps to add as many spreadsheets as you want which will form your workbook.

How to Name Each Spreadsheet that makes a Workbook

By default, when new spreadsheets are added, they are given default names as Sheet1, Sheet2, Sheet3 and so on. If you want to give the individual spreadsheet a unique name, double-click each spreadsheet default name and type the name you want it to bear. After that, click out.

The Quick Access Toolbar Explained

Quick Access Toolbar is located at the top right-hand side of the excel interface, and it contains commands which are used frequently. Using Excel 365 as an example, the commands available in the quick access toolbar are **AutoSave**, **Save**, **Redo** and **Undo** commands.

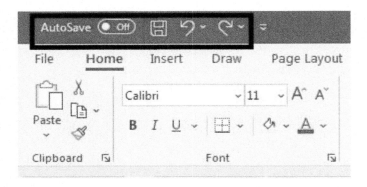

Commands available in Quick Access Toolbar by default indicated in black rectangular shape

Customizing Quick Access Toolbar in Excel

If for instance you frequently use **AutoSum** command which is found in **Formulas** tab, you can add it to the quick access toolbar. To do that, take these steps:

Take your cursor to the command you want to add to quick access toolbar.

Right-click the command.

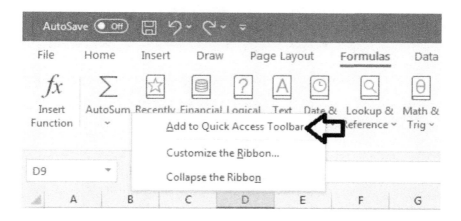

Right-clicking **AutoSum** command that I want to add to **Quick Access Toolbar**

Select the option Add to Quick Access Toolbar.

Immediately you take the last step above, the command is added to **Quick Access Toolbar** and you will see it appear there.

In addition, if you want to delete any command that you initially added to the Quick Access Toolbar section, right-click the command and select **Remove from Quick Access Toolbar**.

Steps in converting Excel Workbook Cells to Table

To convert cells in Microsoft Excel workbook to table, take these steps:

Highlight the cells you want to convert to table format

Click the **Home** tab which is as shown in the picture below:

The **Home** tab shown by the arrow

Click Format as Table **command**

Select the table style you want from the options that will be shown to you

Click **Ok** button of the dialog box

You can then start entering the content you want to have in the table.

How to Sort Items in Excel Workbook

Let me assume that you have list of names in your Excel workbook and you want to sort them alphabetically from A-Z in ascending order. What you need to get the deal done is the **Sort & Filter** command. You do not need to disturb your brain by doing that manually.

To sort the names alphabetically from A to Z, do the following:

Highlight the entire cells containing the words you want to filter

Click the **Home** tab of the workbook

Click the **Sort & Filter** command

Select **Sort A to Z** from the options

If the items you want to sort are group of numbers, when you click the **Sort & Filter** you are to select **Sort Smallest to Largest** or **Sort Largest to Smallest** depending on the result you want.

The Basic Tabs in Excel

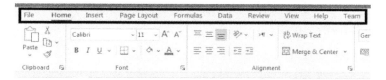

There are basic tabs available in Excel. Through each of these tabs, you can complete specific tasks. The tabs available in the recent version of Excel are **File, Home, Insert, Page Layout, Formulas, Data, Review, View, Help** and **Team**. On your own, you can add other tabs/ribbons of your choice. You can also remove those you do not want to have. I will walk you through on that.

How to Add or Remove Tabs (Ribbons) in Excel

If you want to add or remove tabs in Excel, take these steps:

Click **File** tab

Scroll down and click **Options** commands

Click Customize Ribbon

In the **Main Tabs**, tick the tabs you want to add and click **Ok** button

If your intention is to remove tab, in **Main Tabs**, untick the tab you want to remove and click **Ok** button

Changing Language

Every version of Excel comes with a default language. So, it is left for you to change to any language of your choice.

If you want to change language in Excel, take these steps:

Click **File** tab and followed by **Options**

From the list click **Language**

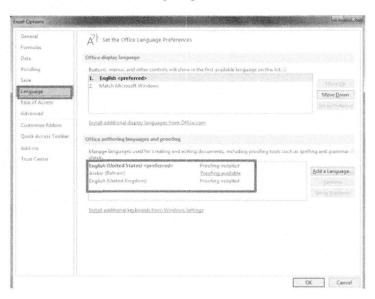

Screen when **Language** is clicked

Under the **Office authoring languages and proofing**, select the language you want to change to and click **Ok** button, but if the language you want to change to is not there, click **Add a language**, select the language from the list that will be shown to you before clicking the **Ok** button.

Know that you have to restart your Excel for the change you made to be effective.

Selecting a Cell

If you want to select a cell, just click on the cell and it is selected. When a cell is selected, it is enclosed in green colored design.

Excel Text Functions

Summary of the TEXT feature in Excel

The TEXT feature in Excel returns a number as text in a defined number format. Can be used The TEXT feature to insert formatted numbers into text.

The goal

In a number format, convert the number to text.

The meaning of the return

In the specified format, a number is a text.

Grammatical structure

(value, format text) =TEXT

Disputes

Price: The amount that needs to be converted.

A number format used is format text.

Iteration

Excel 2003 is a spreadsheet program.

Notes on Application

That TEXT method contains a text-formatted number based on the number format specified. TEXT needs a numeric value as

67

input. TEXT always returns a text string as its output.

Whenever you want to encode (join) a format number to text, the TEXT feature comes in handy. "Sales rose by over $43,500 last year," for example, where the amount 43500 has indeed been configured with a dollar symbol and a thousand separator. The number formatting will be stripped if you don't use the TEXT feature. Times, which appear in large serial numbers, are particularly troublesome. One may embed a number within the text using the same number format you need for TEXT.

a few examples

The TEXT function is being used to format the value in A1 in the examples below:

/ date likes "15-Oct-19" =TEXT(A1,"dd-mmm-yy")

/ percent likes "25 percent " =TEXT (A1,"0 percent ")

"You have won "&TEXT(A1,"$0") / "You have won $100."

Observations:

Custom number formats can be used with the TEXT feature. Format text must be enclosed in double quotes

See Format Cells dialogue box for examples of available number formats.

Excel Date and Time Functions

In Excel, how do I insert the current date and time?

Inserting a current date and time in an Excel spreadsheet can be helpful for those working as just financial analysts. This guide will explain how Excel's current date & time feature functions and provide examples of when it can be helpful in your research.

Formulas for the present date and time in Excel (dynamic)

Depending on the type of data you want to use in your spreadsheet, you can use one of two formulas. These are dynamic formulas, which means they will update every time a spreadsheet is opened.

The formula for calculating the current date:

=RIGHT NOW ()

The formula for current time:

=RIGHT NOW ()

Example of current date & time in Excel

You can see how each works & what the resulting performance is in the screenshot below. For example, if it is May 24, 2019, to 1:36 when you create the formula, the following details will show in your spreadsheet. As Excel outputs the time, it uses a 24-hour clock.

Current Date & Time in Excel

The =TODAY () formula also includes a day when, month, and year, as you can see. More information is shown with the =NOW () feature, which shows the day/ month/year/ hour, & min (using a 24-hour clock).

Formulas for the present date and time in Excel (static)

It's possible that you don't want the figures throughout the file to refresh every time you enter it.

The following are examples of static formulas:

"Ctrl +;" is a shortcut for inserting the date (Windows)

"Ctrl + Shift +;" – this key combination inserts the date & time (Windows)

"COMMAND +;" is a command (Mac)

Why is it essential to include the current date & time in Excel?

You would want to display a current date & time in Excel for a variety of reasons. Let's say you want the current time to be shown on every financial model you print out on the cover page.

There are many reasons to include the time and date:

Keeping track of your activities

On the front page

When printing a text, keep the following in mind:

Version control is essential.

When displaying time-sensitive data

When it comes to taking into account cash flows to present, there are a few things to keep in mind (Present Net Value & XNPV function)

Financial modeling applications

Since time is an essential factor in financial modeling and valuation, the Excel current time & date feature comes in handy when doing financial analysis. The most common application is to discount cash flows and ensure that the present value date becomes right. Depending on the review, you may need to use a static and dynamic version of formulas.

Chapter 4: Personalizing your MS Excel 2022

Excel may be customized in a variety of ways to meet your specific requirements and preferences. You may modify Excel in three ways: (1) using the Quick Access toolbar, (2) changing the default configuration, and (3) using add-ins.

Tailor-fitting the Quick Access Toolbar Excel's Control Panel toolbar, which is placed on the left side of the screen just above the Ribbon, may be customized. The four command buttons are AutoSave, Download, Redo, and Undo.

By right-clicking a Ribbon command button and choosing Add to Quick Access Toolbar from the menu bar; you may add it to the Quick Access toolbar. Excel will immediately move the button to the end of the toolbar.

To move the command button to a new location inside the Quick Access toolbar, click the Customize Control Panel toolbar button, and then More Commands from the dropdown menu.

Adding non-Ribbon commands Other choices, even if they aren't on the Ribbon, maybe added to the Quick Access Toolbar tab.

In the Choose Instructions From list box on the left, choose the command option you wish to add to the Quick Access Toolbar.

To add the selected command button to the bottom of the list box on your right, click the Add button.

To close the dialogue box, click OK.

Exploring your Options

Excel makes assumptions about how you want your spreadsheet and chart data to look on screen and in print whenever you start a new workbook. These statements may not always be accurate. As a result, it's critical that you understand how to use the program's options to get the most out of its capabilities.

User Interface Options

The following boxes and buttons may be found under the User Interface Options:

• Using Multiple Displays – permits you to choose to Optimize for Compatibility so that Excel and other windows on linked display screens seem at their finest.

• Show Mini Bar – hides and re-enables the MiniTool bar, which includes the most crucial Home Tab formatting buttons.

Showing Quick Analysis Options – hides or re-enables the Quick Access toolbar's visibility.

• Enable Live Preview - this option turns on or off the Live Preview functionality.

• ScreenTip Style - alters how the information in ScreenTips is presented.

When Creating New Workbooks

This collection of four combo and text boxes may be found on the Favorites tab of the Excel Options dialogue box: • Use This as the Default Font – put the font name in the combo box to pick a new standard font to use on all worksheet cells.

• Font Size — change the default font size across all worksheets.

• Default View for New Sheets — For all new worksheets, you may choose between Page Break Preview and Page Layout as the default view.

• Include This Many Sheets – in a new workbook, increase or decrease the default number of worksheets (you can put a number between 2 and 225).

Personalize Your Copy of Microsoft Office

There are three possibilities in this section:

• Username – in this text box, you may modify the username that is used as the writer for new Excel workbooks.

• Office Backdrop – This is a dropdown menu that enables you to choose a background pattern for the right side of the application, which displays your Ribbon Display Options, information, and the Restore, Minimize, and Close buttons.

• Office Theme — Choose from Colourful, Light Gray, or White tint choices from this dropdown box.

Start-Up Options

The following options are available in the Start-Up Options section:

• Selecting Extensions to Open by Default in Excel — When you click the Default Programs button, a Set Links for the Program dialogue box appears, allowing you to choose the kinds of application files you wish to be associated with the program. To open Excel, double-click any file with the desired extension.

• Tell Me if Microsoft Excel Isn't the Default Software for Viewing/Editing Spreadsheets - this option controls whether or not you are notified if an Excel workbook file is connected with another spreadsheet program or viewer.

• When the Application Starts, Show the Start Screen – This box controls whether the Start screen shows when you begin Excel.

Calculation Options

You can adjust when formulae in your worksheet are recalculated and how an equation that Excel cannot answer on the first attempt is recalculated using the Calculation Options.

• Autonomous Except for Data Tables – This option causes Excel to recalculate formulae except for those input into the What-if data tables. To update formulae, go to the Formulas tab and select Calculate Now (F9) or Calculate Sheet (Shift +F9).

• Manual – this choice button enables entire manual recalculation, which means that formulae that need to be updated are only recalculated when you use the Calculate Now or Calculate Sheet commands.

• Activate Iterative Calculation - this option allows you to enable or deactivate iterative calculations for formulae that Excel couldn't solve the first time around.

• Maximum Iterations - alter the number of times Excel computes an insolvable calculation in this text box.

• Maximum Alter – increase the amount by which Excel raises its estimate value when trying to calculate a formula in an effort to solve it in this text box.

Working with Formulas Options

There are four checkboxes in the Working on Formulas Options section that include formula-related options: • R1C1 Reference Style – this option allows or inhibits the R1C1 cell reference system, which assigns R45C2 for cell B45 to columns and rows.

• Formula Autocorrect – disables or re-enables Excel's Formula AutoComplete feature, which attempts to finish the formula or function you're manually modifying.

• User Table Names in Equations – to turn off and on the functionality that uses range names you've established in a table of data.

• Use GetPivotData Methods for PivotTable References – this toggles the GetPivotTable function, which Excel uses to obtain data from different fields in a data source, on or off.

Error Checking and Error Checking Rules

You can handle error-checking for formulae using the other settings on a Formulas tab of the Options dialogue.

The lone check box in the Error Checking section is Enable Background Error Testing, which enables you to run error checks in the background while doing other Excel operations.

When an equation relates to an empty cell, the Mistake Checking Rules check for a formula error.

Data Options

There are four checkboxes in the Data Options section of the Data tab. These settings let you customize how Excel manages large volumes of data that can be accessed through external data searches or Excel's pivot table functionality.

When updating data in a pivot table from data sources with 300,000 or more rows, Excel disables the undo capability.

Simply deselect the Disable Undo for Big PivotTable Refresh Actions check box for all refresh activities in large pivot tables.

Simply uncheck the Disable Undo for Large Data Model Operations option to activate the Undo functionality for any operations involving data lists.

AutoCorrect Options

There are four tabs in the AutoCorrect Options dialogue box:

• AutoCorrect – determines which corrections Excel does automatically.

• AutoFormat As You Type - checkboxes that regulate whether or not hyperlinks are used to substitute Internet addresses or network routes.

• Actions - Activate a date or financial sign context menu when you put in a specific date or economic text in the cells by enabling Additional Actions.

• Arithmetic AutoCorrect — Using the Replace and With text box, you may replace specific text on your worksheet with math symbols.

Modifying Save Options on the Save Tab

Under the Save tab's choices, there are four sections:

• Save Workbooks,

• AutoRecover, and Exceptions for the current workbook.

- Document Management Server Files Offline Editing Options

- Maintain the Workbook's Visual Appearance

Customizing the Excel Ribbon

You may alter which tabs appear on the Excel Ribbon and in what order they appear, as well as adjust which sets of command buttons appear on each of the tabs, using the Customize Ribbon tab of Excel Options. You can also use these options to create new Ribbon tabs and custom groups of command buttons inside the tabs that are already shown.

Customizing Ribbon tabs

If you wish to change the default layout of the primary tabs and groups on the Excel Ribbon, you may do so by doing the following steps: Deselect their checkboxes in the Main Tabs list box on the right side of the Excel Options to hide tabs on the Ribbon.

Select the tab to move and then click Move Up or Move Down until the name of the tab appears in the desired location on the Ribbon.

To change the order of the groups, use the Extend button to expand the tab to the display groups. After that, click the name of the group you want to move and drag it up or down the list until it appears in the appropriate location.

Remove a group from a tab by selecting it from the expand Main Tabs list and clicking the Remove command button.

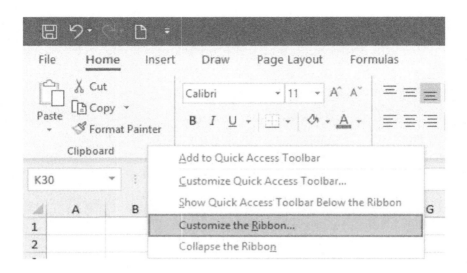

Using Office Add-ins

Excel supports Office Add-ins to help build your worksheets. These are small app programs that run within specific Office 2019 applications, including Excel, and increase certain functions and boost productivity.

To use Office Add-ins, you have to install them via the following steps:

1. Click the My Add-ins option found in the Insert tab of the Ribbon, then select the See All option on the dropdown menu.

2. Click the Store button in the Office Add-ins dialog box to connect to the Office Store.

3. Click desired Office Add-in to purchase (some add-ins are free), then install.

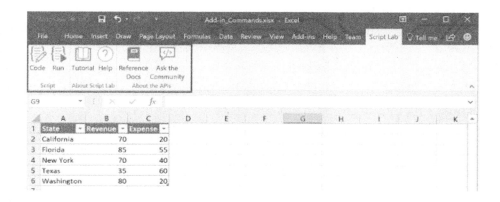

Chapter 5: Mastering Worksheets and Workbooks in MS Excel 2022

Since you've mastered Excel 2022's simple menus and features, it's time to fill out a worksheet of details to see how Excel does it. When you hear the word "spreadsheet" about Excel, you most likely think about an Excel spreadsheet. Microsoft, on the other hand, distinguishes between worksheets and workbooks.

Worksheets vs. Workbooks

It might sound like a minor differentiation, but knowing the difference between a worksheet and a workbook in Excel is critical when dealing with equations and linked data. A new workbook is created when you generate a new Excel file. A file created with MS excel is generally known as a workbook.

Excel 2022 dynamically installs a fresh sheet when you build a workbook. The title of the sheet can be found in the bottom-left corner of the opened workbook slot.

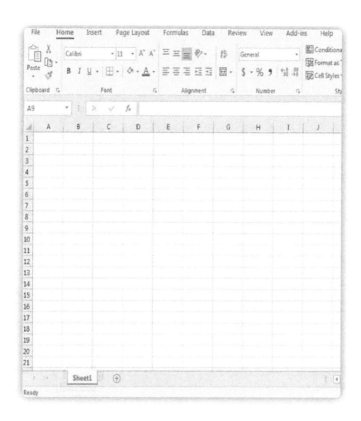

(One worksheet in an Excel workbook)

Each sheet in the workbook may be used to store data ordered by category, and each sheet can connect to other sheets in the workbook. For example, a workbook called "Customer Orders" may have two sheets. Customer delivery information is on one sheet, and order information is on the other. To decide the address to submit merchandise, a worksheet of customer orders will refer to a worksheet of customer shipping details.

Keep an eye out for the "+" symbol next to the sheet in the graphic. When you click it, a new sheet with the following numerical value in the name is formed. "Sheet1" is the default label for the first stack. The next sheet title is "Sheet2," as you make a new sheet. And if you choose the default names for the worksheets, each worksheet in an Excel 2022 workbook must have its name.

You are not required to use the default tag. The name of a worksheet may be modified. Excel will ask you to give it a new name when you double-click "Sheet1" on the first worksheet page. The name you type in the text box would be added to your worksheet. The worksheet's name is changed to this current name. You must assign each of your Worksheets its name so that you can only provide unique worksheet names.

Below are the ways through which a user can access the pre-stored workbooks on a computer or device:

Click File ⇨ Open ⇨ Recent and pick from the collection on the right of the File you like. This just shows the most commonly used files.

From the Advanced settings available under the "option," a user can set the custom number of excel files to view (the maximum limit is 50).

Click Open File and select a position from the list on the left. Sites differ based on which "sites" you have set up. You can see Cloud-based options.

Some of the alternatives are usually This Computer. With the folder, you can go straight to the folders or press Browse to open the Open dialog box, allowing you even more choices.

Locate the Excel workbook file from a complete list of files in the Data Explorer. Just double-click on the folder (or icon), and Excel opens the workbook. When Excel is not operating, Windows must launch Excel immediately and upload the document to the workbook.

Save a Workbook

Your workbook is open to day-ruining incidents like power failures and machine crashes while working in Excel. And you should permanently save your work.

Excel is providing four ways to preserve the workbook:

Tap the Save button in the toolbar for Quick Control. (It's like an old-fashioned floppy disk.)

Tap Ctrl+S.

Tap Shift+F12.

Use the File ⇨ Save option.

When the workbook has already been stored, it will be updated at the same place again with the same filename. When the user wants to move the workbook to a new file or venue, click Move as File (or press F12).

The option with Save As dialog box matches the Open dialog window. Pick the appropriate tab on the left-hand side of the tab tree. On choosing the tab, type the filename in the field FileName. You don't have to define a file extension — Excel will automatically update it, depending on the type of File defined in the Save as File field. For example, files are stored in the regular Excel file format that uses an extension of.xlsx.

Unless the position you choose already holds a file of the same title, Excel asks if the user wants to replace the File with the current one. Be alert! Once you delete it, you cannot restore the original File.

Auto Recover

When you have been using computers for some amount of time, you certainly have missed any work. If you did not save your work, or maybe electricity failure occurs, you will lose the unsaved work. Or perhaps you worked on something and didn't think it was relevant, so you closed the File without saving it. Of course, you

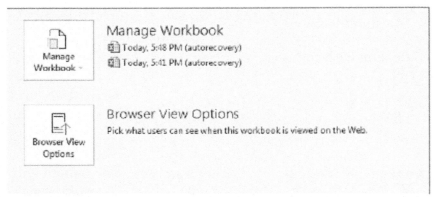

learned later that this was necessary too. The functionality of Auto Recover available in MS Excel could extract such "d' oh" forms! " in rare instances.

When you work in Excel, your job is stored automatically daily.

This is all in the distance, and you don't even know it's going on. A user can view and retrieve the autosaved files in MS excel if appropriate. This option works for the file you never save during your work and excel save them temporarily in the backend.

Two parts form the Auto Recover feature: The Excel Workbook copies are stored in a temp folder automatically for retrieval in case of sudden failure of program or loss of power to the computer; these files are deleted once the main file is closed or saved by the user.

Workbooks, where you have shut without saving, will be stored as draft copies.

Configuring Auto Recover: Auto Recover files are usually saved after 10 minutes. It is preferred to change the time settings under the Save tab available under the "Options" dialog box of the MS excel. You should assign a one-to-one minute, saving time.

When dealing with confidential information, you may choose not to store previous copies on your computer immediately. The Save tabs in your Excel Options dialog box help you to thoroughly uninstall this function or uninstall it for a particular workbook only.

Password-Protecting a Workbook

In certain instances, you may like to have your workbook password specified. If the file is needed to be open, then the user must 1st verify the password, and then it can be opened.

Follow these steps to set a Workbook password: 1. Use File ⇨ Info and press the button Protect Workbook. This button shows a few more choices in a dropdown column.

2. From the list, pick Encrypt with Password. The MS Excel shows the option for Encrypt File, which is given as under.

3. Type the name, press OK, and then re-enter.

4. Select OK and then close your workbook after saving.

When the workbook is reopened, you will be asked for a password.

This option is available where a user creates a password for the file.

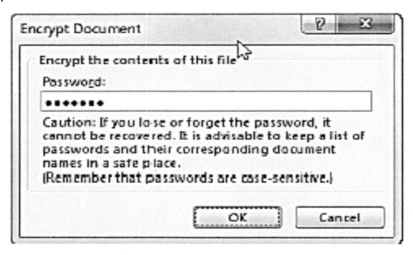

Entering Data in a Worksheet

Once you've established your worksheet, you should start filling in the cells. Since Excel 2022 has too many formatting options, this segment focuses on the fundamentals of inputting information and dealing with alphanumeric values rather than formulas and numbers.

Launch a worksheet and type the following information into cells A1 and B1: *5*

Note that the first column is labeled "A," and the second column is labeled "B." Since row number "1" appears in both cells, you realize the data must be inserted in the first row.

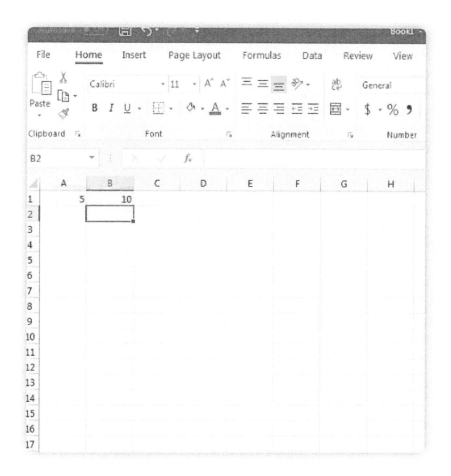

(*Cells A1 and B1 have data entered into them.*) Cell C1 can now be filled with the value "001." Excel 2022 removes the zeros from the value and shows "1" in the cell. This is how Excel tries to figure out what kind of data is in a cell and formats it accordingly.

Unfortunately, Excel does not often correctly evaluate the data form and wrongly shows figures. You can circumvent Excel's default behavior and compel it to show values precisely as you join them using a feature provided by Microsoft.

Return to C1 and shift "001" to "001" as your input (notice the single tick mark in front of the first zero). The single tick mark instructs Excel to avoid specifying the data form and instead show the data as entered.

You'll note that your spreadsheet already shows 001 without the zeros being removed by Excel. You should still apply a single tick character to interrupt the automatic formatting if you reach data that isn't formatted correctly.

You may want to use an estimate in a cell on occasion. If you have many figures that you cannot insert without a calculator, you can use Excel's internal calculator to solve the problem for you.

The equal sign (=) is used to mean that a measurement should be performed in a cell. The opportunity to use formulas and equations is that any critical factor to choosing Excel 2022 over some other data storage program. Excel is ideal for equations ranging from simple adding and subtracting to complicated formulas, including arithmetic so that you can do the same behavior with most other office applications. Getting to know how to convert a simple math equation to Excel "English" is the most challenging aspect of using Excel for these calculations.

Insert the equal sign at the start of your data entry for simple measures. Insert the following data into cell D1 of your spreadsheet: =4+3

We want to include the numbers 4 and 3 in the illustration above. You aren't restricted to only two numbers, and you can measure any amount of values.

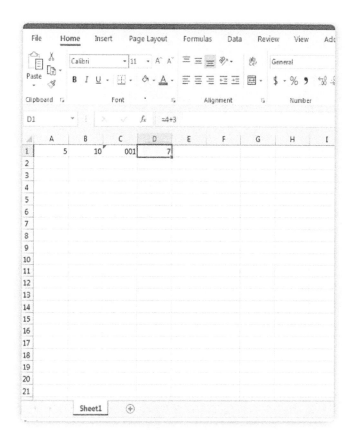

(Cell D1 contains a calculation to bring the numbers 4 and 3 together) Note how the value "7" appears in cell D1, although the value entered was "=4+3." As Excel 2022 completes a measurement, the outcome is shown. To see the equation in the text area underneath the menu, click the cell.

You may make a measurement error. For example, if you type a letter rather than a number in a cell, Excel would detect the mistake. Excel 2022 shows a note where there is a flaw in the equation, so it can't figure out how to display the data.

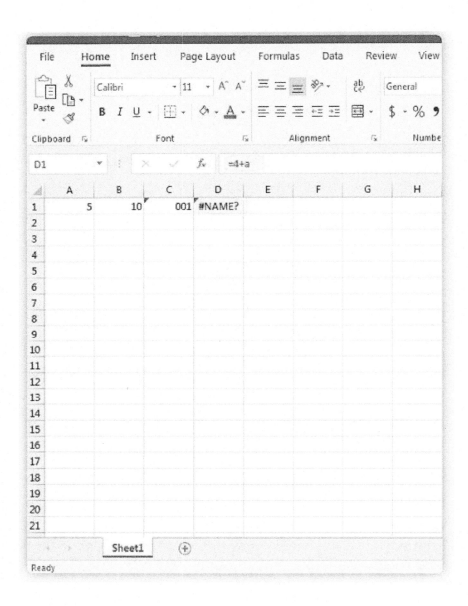

(A mistake in a math equation is shown above) The character "a" is used in the math equation instead of the number "3." Excel doesn't know what to do with a letter because it can't be included in an

equation, so it shows "#NAME?" in the active cell. This is how you will discover if there is a problem with the estimate.

Use of Calculation and Making Reference for Other Cells

MS Excel has features that enable you to dynamically measure values in cells depending on the data you join. This is accomplished by entering values into cells and afterward displaying the effects in a different cell. Remove all of the data from the latest spreadsheet. Replace 5 with 10 in A1 and B1 with the values and cells from the previous case.

Assume the user wants to run a calculation with the values in A1 and B1 and show the results in C1. The A1 and B1 codes may be used to refer to the two meanings. Join the following formula in cell C1: =A1+B1

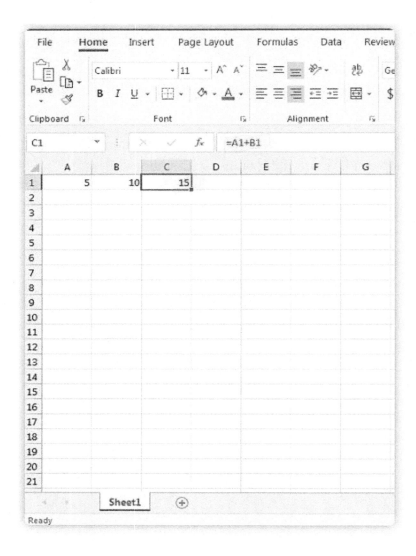

(Two external cells are used in the calculations) You even use the equal sign to inform Excel that you'd like to perform a calculation using cells besides the active one, so rather than using static

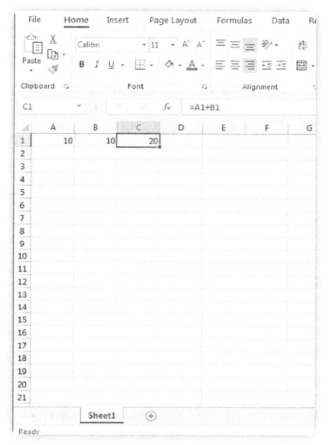

numbers, you just use cell term. You may now apply new data to cells referenced by name, and the referencing cell can instantly recalculate the results. Adjust the number "5" in A1 to "10" in the same spreadsheets.

(C1 recalculates changes in inserted values) Excel senses the shift and recalculates the equation now that the value "5" has been modified to "10." The value 20 is now shown in cell C1 in this case. The text inserted into C1 has not been altered in any way. It's the same because it also refers to the same cell names. However, the

shown value has been revised to represent the most recent estimates. The advantage of Excel 2022 is that this operation is performed automatically. There is no need to manually update results or press some keys. When you change the values of the spreadsheet, all of your calculations and equations can dynamically refresh.

There are some advantages of dynamic patches and recalculations. Include the case that you ought to keep a record of your monthly expenditures. You'll need three separate estimates to figure out how much you pay for food, shopping, and petrol. An Excel spreadsheet with three cells that relate data to three other cells can be developed. The measurements will be done automatically when you insert new values per month when you enter various details.

Assume you have many cells to be used in your equation, and typing them all may result in typos. To include each cell in the equation, press it with the cursor. In cell F1 of the same spreadsheet, insert the number "5". Then press C1, which would be the cell where the effects of the calculation are shown.

Insert the plus sign into the equation, and then press F1 on the keyboard. You'll see that Excel applies the cell mark F1 to your formula automatically.

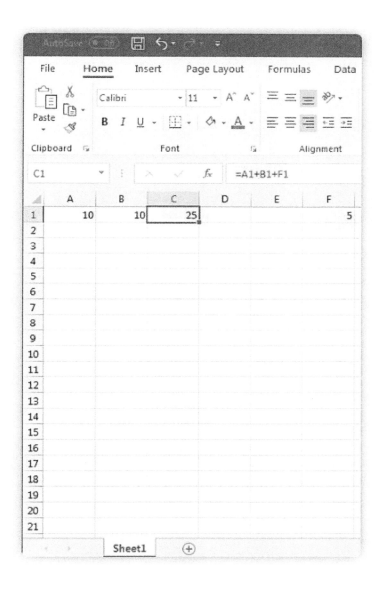

(Third Cell inserted in an Excel equation) Using the mouse, you will apply several cells to the equation at once. Keep the CTRL

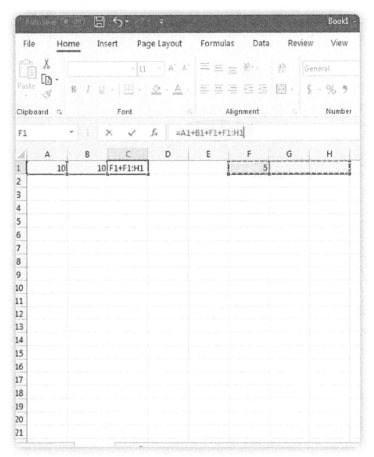

keyboard key when adding another plus symbol to the active cell. Select all of the cells you choose to be used in the equation using your mouse press.

(Adding several cells to a calculation) The colon character is used to denote the number of cells in Excel. The range F1 to H1 is included in this example's estimate. All data entered in these cells would be used in the final result. If no data is inserted into these cells, Excel considers them zero, and the figures remain unchanged.

You'll see more models and equations when you deal with more details in Excel. They can be incorporated into diagrams and maps. Instead of typing each cell separately, connecting several cells to a calculation with the mouse requires just a few seconds. Build easy spreadsheets that monitor your data using these fundamental techniques.

Three Types of Data

Text, value, and formula data are the three categories of data in Excel 2022. This is the kind of information you put into cells. If Excel recognizes the submission as a formula, the formula would be calculated and the outcome shown in the cell. When the cell is involved, you could see the formula inside the Formula Bar.

If Excel senses that it isn't a calculation, it determines if it is text or meaning. The text inputs are oriented to the cell's left edge. Right-hand values are matched.

This information is essential to ensure that you are entering data correctly and that Excel 2022 recognizes your entries as the correct data sort.

Text Data

Text entries are all pieces of information that Excel can't define as a formula or a meaning. The majority of the text entries are labeled. Row and column labels are the titles of the rows and columns.

If Excel categorizes the data as text, the text would always be offset to the left side of the cell.

Values

Values are the fundamental components of all formulas you join. Values are figures that describe amounts as well as dates.

The cell's values are matched on the right edge.

Excel can say the values you apply as formula are values if it can't solve them.

Adding Values

Let's look at how to type data into an Excel spreadsheet.

▢ *Negative values:* If you need to incorporate a negative value, precede it with a minus (-) symbol. If you like, you can even use parentheses. If you use brackets, Excel can translate them to a negative value.

▢ *Dollar amounts:* You should apply dollar signs and commas to any value that is a dollar sum, much like you do if you're composing it by hand.

▢ *Decimal points:* Just use the period key with your keyboard to insert a decimal point.

▢ *Fractions:* There's no reason to worry whether you need to translate a fraction to decimal because Excel will do that for you. Simply use the slash key on the keyboard to enter the fraction. Merely leave a gap after some whole numbers before typing in the fraction, as seen in the example below.

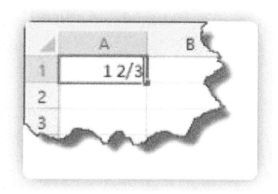

On your keyboard, press Enter.

Excel defined the number as a value and matched this to the right, as seen below. It is, though, just a tiny percentage.

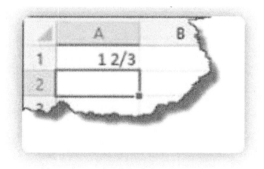

I am looking at the Formula Bar after clicking on the cell that holds the fraction.

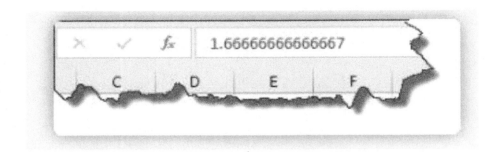

It was translated to a decimal by Excel.

Remember: If a whole number isn't available in a clear fraction, such as 5/8, you must enter a zero as the entire number. Excel 2022 assumes you're hitting a deadline if you don't.

Formulas

A formula in Excel is just an equation, which conducts a calculation. This may be as easy as 3 + 5 or as complicated as $(3 + 5)16 \div 3\pi$. You may do calculations in a solo cell, a series of cells (blocks), or even a set of cells through several worksheets. A chosen block or community of cells or blocks is referred to as a set of cells. Don't panic if this is all a little overwhelming right now. It will quickly become clear.

For the time being, note that every formula you enter into Excel 2022 must begin with an equality symbol: =. This can seem odd initially since an equality symbol typically appears after a mathematical equation, but it informs Excel that you would like to run a measurement right away. When the user wants to insert a formula to Excel, always begin using the equality sign, as seen

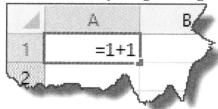

below:

Press Enter or even the arrow key after you has inserted it into your cell to move to a different cell.

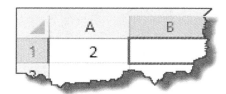

Excel completes the equation and shows the result in the appropriate cell.

Your formula will then appear in your Formula Bar if you click on the cell.

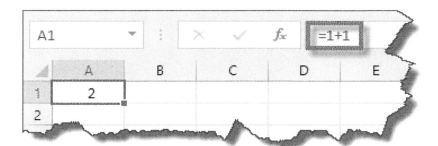

Adjusting your Decimal Points

Suppose user really needs to join a series of numbers with the fixed amount of decimal points. In that case, they could custom Excel's Fixed Decimal option to get your decimal point added automatically.

To do so, liveliness to the offstage region to click the File button, then Options.

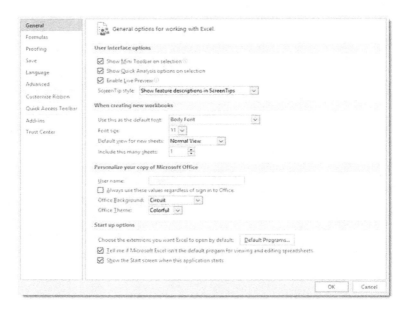

Select Advanced from the left-hand side.

Go to the Automatically section. Place a check inside the box and insert a decimal point.

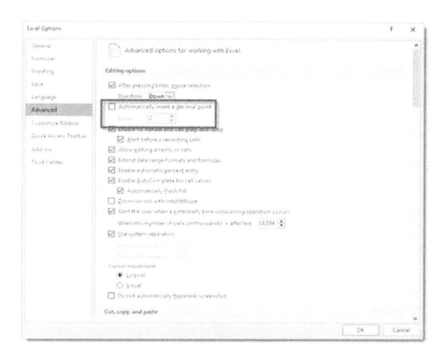

It is fixed to two positions from the right by design. If necessary, you may adjust this amount.

Adding Dates

Time and date in your worksheet are values and not text input. They are numeric values, and they may be found in formulas, such as determining how many days a week a worker spent in the previous month. In other words, Excel 2022 recognizes when you are accessing a time or date based on how you enter it.

The following are the methods for entering a period into Excel such that it is recognized as a value and not text:

AM or 3 PM

A or 3 P

3:45 AM or 3:45 PM

3:45:12 AM or 3:45:12 PM

15:45

15:45:12

The date syntax that you are Excel 2022 considers as values are mentioned below:

June 1, 2020, or June 1, 20. It'll show up in Excel as 1-June-20.

5/6/20 or 5-6-20. It'll show up in Excel as 5/6/2020.

3-June-20 or 3/June/20 or 3June20. It'll show up in Excel as 3-June-2020.

June-3 or June/3 or June 3 It'll show up in Excel as 3-June.

Please keep in mind: If the ending two digits of your year are 00-29, you need to reach the last two digits of the year for this era. You must insert all four numbers opening with 2030.

Entering Data in a Worksheet

It is time to start inserting data into Excel now that we have discussed specific fundamentals of data. It is as simple as pressing on a cell to enter data. Your cell will be illuminated with an outline when you press on it, as seen below.

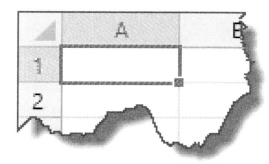

You may type inside it until it's outlined with a border. You can press your mouse into a different cell to enter more details after typing data into one cell.

Moving and tapping the mouse every time you choose to switch cells, on the other hand, becomes tedious. Most Excel 2022 users tend to work a bit quicker to save as much effort as you can. However, you could use the subsequent keys to access the spreadsheet when entering data.

⬜ *Enter:* Moves the cursor to the next cell in the same column after entering the data in the current cell. In other terms, pressing 'Enter' in the illustration above will shift the selection down and select cell A2. Therefore, we should enter cell A2.

⬜ *Tab:* Tab pushes one cell over in the same row after entering data in the current section. It will switch to B1 in this case.

⬜ *Arrows:* By using arrows, you will move around the spreadsheet's columns and rows.

⬜ *Esc:* Removes the latest entry from the list.

Labels for Rows and Column's

Labels are utilized to mark columns that contain details and descriptions, headings, and names. Text values are what these are.

Here is the start of your spreadsheet that would be utilized to measure the monthly revenue for every employee.

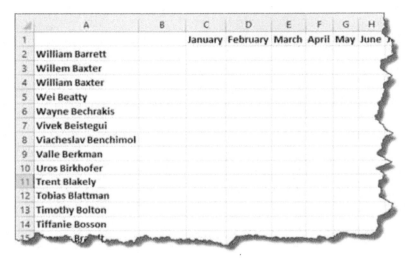

Excel accepted our submissions as some text values, as you have seen. The text values are still matched to the cell's left edge.

Repeated labels: Let us assume we need to use William Barrett's first name two times in the spreadsheet.

Using the Pick List function to insert frequent labels easily is a good option—Right-click on your cell where you would like a title to display to use the Pick List function. 'Pick from a Dropdown option' should be selected.

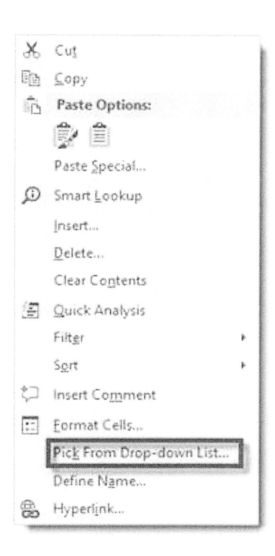

A dropdown menu will appear when we click on Choose from

Dropdown option:

By clicking on the mark we want to appear, we will make it appear.

In our case, we'd scroll down before we came across William Barrett, then press on his profile. In the cell, the text mark William Barrett has now been reached.

Closing a Workbook

You should close it when you are done with a workbook to release the space it uses. Other workbooks are expected to stay available. You close Excel as well as exit the very last open workbook.

You will exit a workbook with any of the options below:

Pick File ⇨ Close. Click the Close button (X) in the right corner of the title bar of the browser.

Hit Ctrl+F4.

Hit Ctrl+W.

Whether you have made some changes to the workbook since it was last updated, Excel will inquire if you would like to restore the modifications to the workbook before closing.

Working with Templates

In general, a prototype is a pattern that acts as a basis for another. An Excel blueprint is usually a specific type of file used as a premade or preformatted document for working with other worksheets. Excel provides you some of the premade templates, or a user can make their own; doing so will require you to invest some time, but it will surely save you a lot of time later on.

Exploring Excel Templates: The easiest way to familiarize you with the Excel sample files is to hop in and check out others. Excel 2022 offers timely access to hundreds of prototype files.

Viewing Templates: Use File ⇨ new to use the Excel models.

The prototype thumbnails that show on the screen are only a small selection of the ones available. Select one of your search words listed, or type in a specific term and check for more.

Enter the invoice, for instance, and press the Search button. Several thumbnails are shown in Excel. You may use the group filters on the right to narrow down the results. Given below is a sample invoice template.

Creating a Workbook from a Template

To build a template-based workbook, find a prototype that seems like it could be doing the job and tap on the thumbnail. Excel shows a box that includes a bigger version, the template source, and some extra material. If it still looks nice, press the key Build. If not, tap on one of your arrows to see information for the next (or previous) design in the list.

Clicking the Create button will allow Excel to import the prototype and then build a new workbook focused on that design. The operation you perform may vary according to the template. That prototype is specific, but much of it is self-explanatory. Many workbooks include tailoring. Substitute the details default with your own.

The following Figure shows a workbook built from a blueprint. In some ways, this workbook requires to be personalized. Once the template is used again, customizing it is more effective than any workbook generated from the template.

A workbook created from a template.

Use the save command for later use of this document. Excel provides a filename based on the prototype title, so you can choose whatever filename you choose.

Using Default Templates: Excel provides three types of using the file: the original template for the workbook. This type is being used as the base for new workbooks. The default template, which is used as a base for later use while working with other files.

These premade files of templates include formals that can be used while working with other files. It will help you to save time and work effortlessly.

Printing Your Work

The "quick print" provides the user ability to print the current file fast and effortlessly. One way to trigger this control is to pick the Print file (which shows the backstage view display pane) and press the print button. The Ctrl+P keyboard shortcut will have the same impact as the [Print] file. Using Ctrl+P to display the backstage view, the emphasis is on the Print button, and you can only click Enter to print.

If you like the concept of printing with one click, take a few moments to insert a new button into your Quick Access toolbar. Click the down-pointing arrow on the right-hand side of your Quick Access toolbar and then pick Quick Print from the dropdown column. Excel attaches the button on Fast Print to the Easy Access toolbar.

Simply click the Fast Print button will print the latest worksheet, using the same print settings on the currently selected printer. If a user changes the print settings in the template file, then new settings will be used for printing; otherwise, the default settings for the print will be used by MS excel.

Prints the current worksheet (or all chosen worksheets) plus any maps or items inserted.

Prints one copy.

Prints in portrait mode

Prints the full working worksheet

It doesn't scale the printed output

Utilizes text-size paper with borders of 0.75 inches for top and bottom and margins of 0.70 inches from left and right margins (for the U.S. version)

Prints without headers and footers

Doesn't print comments attached to a cell?

Prints without cell gridlines

Prints down and then over with wider worksheets that cover several pages.

When printing a worksheet, Excel only prints the active area of your Worksheet. In other words, it isn't going to print all 17 billion cells — just those with data present in them. This option will print any object which is hidden in excel including smart art or any other object.

Chapter 6: Tools Used in MS Excel 2022

Sorting Data

In MS Excel, sorting data rearranges the rows depending on the contents of a certain column. Sorting a table to place names in alphabetical order is a good idea. Alternatively, you might arrange data by Amount from smallest to greatest or from biggest to smallest.

Here's an example of a table with carelessly organized records. The states aren't in alphabetical order, and the months aren't in chronological order.

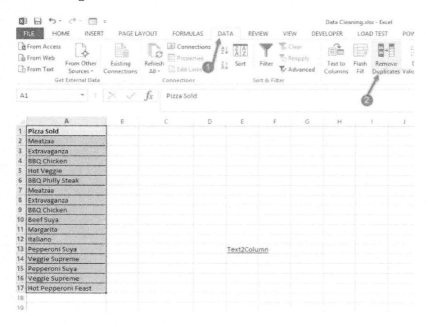

Let's start by sorting the data by state alphabetically. The steps for sorting a table are outlined below. Choose the table, then select Sort & Filter from the Home menu. A sorting dialogue box appears.

This dialogue box enables you to add more than one level of sorting to the usual one. In the Sort by box, choose "State" and "A to Z" in the Order box. The final product may be seen below.

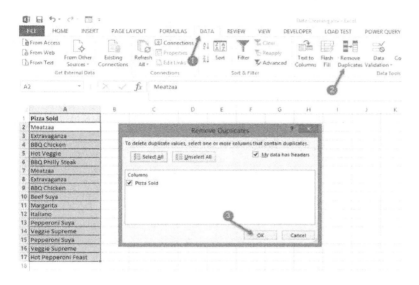

In the sorting dialogue box, you may add an additional level of sorting. This would be beneficial for sorting tables such as those used in national population censuses. You may choose to arrange by state first (from Abia to Zamfara) and then by Local Government Areas. As a result, you'll have a configuration similar to the one shown below. The next step isto arrange the months in the natural sequence that we are used to – January to December. This will need a form of sorting known as "Left to Right," as opposed to the "Top to Bottom" sorting we just completed.

To do this, we begin by selecting the table from the first to the final month. We'll keep the state field blank since we want it to stay in its current condition. Then, on the month-by-month row (Row 2), change the order from Oldest to Newest. The end product is seen below.

Filtering Data

Filtering Filter is one of the most often used tools among Excel power users. It lets you pick what parts of a table you wish to see and conceal the rest.

It's really simple to use and can be accessed from three distinct Excel locations. Filter may be accessed by right-clicking and choosing Filter. Select Sort & Filter from the Home menu on the right. From the Data dropdown menu. You'll notice a dropdown box beside the table headings after you've switched on the Filter tool by clicking on it. By selecting the dropdown box, you may see all of the unique items in that area and choose which ones you wish to see (hiding the rest). All things are chosen by default, so you'll have to deselect the ones you don't want to view. Except for the BBQ Chicken, all of the pizza toppings were left unselected in the screenshot below (meaning only BBQ Chicken was selected). The blue row numbers are Excel's method of graphically indicating that certain rows have been buried since they do not include the things we wish to look at.

S/N	Pizza Sold	Time
3	BBQ Chicken	8:00:04 AM
50	BBQ Chicken	8:01:34 AM
71	BBQ Chicken	8:02:06 AM
74	BBQ Chicken	8:02:13 AM
83	BBQ Chicken	8:02:37 AM
91	BBQ Chicken	8:02:49 AM
168	BBQ Chicken	8:05:23 AM
176	BBQ Chicken	8:05:34 AM
181	BBQ Chicken	8:05:39 AM
182	BBQ Chicken	8:05:40 AM
196	BBQ Chicken	8:06:01 AM
198	BBQ Chicken	8:06:03 AM
205	BBQ Chicken	8:06:22 AM
213	BBQ Chicken	8:06:40 AM
215	BBQ Chicken	8:06:46 AM
231	BBQ Chicken	8:07:07 AM
242	BBQ Chicken	8:07:28 AM
266	BBQ Chicken	8:08:31 AM
275	BBQ Chicken	8:08:45 AM
276	BBQ Chicken	8:08:45 AM
316	BBQ Chicken	8:09:55 AM

Filtering is as simple as that.

Data Cleaning

A lot of the time, the data you're given to work within Excel isn't in a format you can work withandhasto becleanedupbeforeyou canproceedwiththestudyyou planned. Most of the time, you'll have to manually clean the data and correct any faults it has one by one before moving on to the original study you planned to run on it. Fortunately,Excel offersanumberofuseful featuresthatmay assistyou inautomating portions of the data cleansing process.

Removing duplicates and Text to Columns are two of the most prevalent. Then we'll go through a unique tool that may assist you in quickly categorizing your data: Substantial. Finally, we'll look at Data Validation, a clever technique for eliminating data input mistakes in Excel spreadsheets.

Getting Rid of Duplicates

You may sometimes have a table where you wish to eliminate duplicate entries. If it were a sales transaction table, the duplicate sales entries could be removed. It's a table of things (Pizzas) in the example below, and we want to delete the duplicate entries so that only unique elements remain. As seen above, you select all of the records first, then go to the Data menu and choose to Remove Duplicates. A confirmation dialogue box will appear. Click the OK button. The number of duplicate values identified and the number of unique values identified will be shown as a result. Remove Duplicates basically leaves one record for each item and deletes all the additional records it finds for that item.

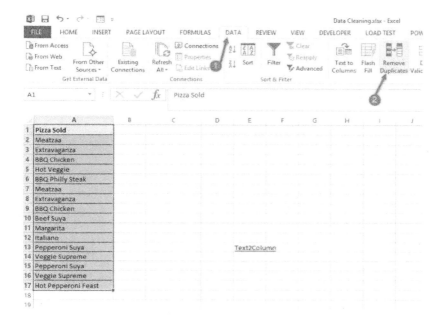

When you pick a table with multiple field entries, the Remove Duplicates command removes only entries that have the same value in all fields as a previous item, unless you specify specific fields to exclude from the duplicate search.

We removed Car Sales from the fields to include in the duplicates search in the screenshot below. As a result, all rows except one will be eliminated if they contain identical entries in all other fields.

	A	B	C	D	E
1	Car Make	Car Sales	Uche & Sons Autodealership	C Davies Cars Ltd	Bello & Bello Ltd
2	France	Bugatti	25	25	33
3	France	Peugeot	20	5	25
4	France	Renault	24	24	31
5	Germany	BMW			33
6	Germany	Porsche			14
7	Germany	Audi			13
8	Germany	Volksw			11
9	Germany	Merced			34
10	Germany	Opel			41
11	India	Tata			7
12	India	Ashok			13
13	India	Mahind			15
14	Italy	Masera			9
15	Italy	Lambor			27
16	Japan	Toyota			10
17	Japan	Honda			12
18	Japan	Honda			34
19	Japan	Mazda	22	5	25
20	Japan	Nissan	11	36	6
21	Japan	Isuzu	44	15	34
22	Japan	Infiniti	8	18	28

Remove Duplicates   ?   ×

To delete duplicate values, select one or more columns that contain duplicates.

[Select All]   [Unselect All]   ☑ My data has headers

Columns
☑ Car Make
☐ Car Sales
☑ Uche _Sons Autodealership
☑ C Davies Cars Ltd
☑ Bello _Bello Ltd

[OK]   [Cancel]

Columns to Text

There can be occasions when you have data that you would rather be divided over numerous columns than crammed into one. This often occurs when you transfer data into Excel from an external source or open data produced from other company applications such as CRMs and ERPs. If there is a distinguishable character dividing each field or they have predetermined lengths per field, Excel's Text to Columns tool is the magic tool for dividing such data inputs into many columns. A basic example of separating a whole name into first and last name fields in one column is shown below. The delimited option specifies that each field is separated by a recognized character. Every initial name and surname name are separated by a space in this example. When you pick the suitable delimiter, Excel displays a line between the first and last names (space, in this case). After that, click Next and Finish.

 Subtotal is a well-kept Excel trick for quickly analyzing a table. It categorizes the data and groups it into groups that offer you varying degrees of information. It's also quite simple to operate. We'll utilize it in the example below.

	Car Make	Car Sales	Uche & Sons Autodealership	C Davies Cars Ltd	Bello & Bello Ltd
1	Car Make	Car Sales	Uche & Sons Autodealership	C Davies Cars Ltd	Bello & Bello Ltd
2	France	Bugatti	25	25	33
3	France	Peugeot	20	5	25
4	France	Renault	24	24	31
5	Germany	BMW	20	6	33
6	Germany	Porsche	27	45	14
7	Germany	Audi	28	43	43
8	Germany	Volkswagen	16	43	11
9	Germany	Mercedes-Benz	23	45	34
10	Germany	Opel	24	16	41
11	India	Tata	41	29	7
12	India	Ashok Leyland	41	19	13
13	India	Mahindra	34	27	15
14	Italy	Maserati	13	22	9
15	Italy	Lamborghini	31	26	27
16	Japan	Toyota	30	24	40
17	Japan	Honda	11	42	12
18	Japan	Honda	36	31	34
19	Japan	Mazda	22	5	25
20	Japan	Nissan	11	36	6
21	Japan	Isuzu	44	15	34
22	Japan	Infiniti	8	18	28
23	Japan	Datsun	31	18	11
24	Japan	Subaru	24	7	20
25	Japan	Suzuki	13	29	43
26	Japan	Scion	26	18	36
27	South Korea	Hyundai	32	28	40

It's a market research data table that displays the various automobile brands offered at three distinct auto dealerships. We can do some interesting analysis by applying a subtotal to this.Choose the table, then select Subtotal from the Data menu. Tick all the fields that contain numeric values (excluding those that you don't want to see a numeric analysis of) in the "Add subtotal to" portion of the dialogue box that appears.

Now that you've been taught illustrated data cleaning, here are a few tips for you to keep your excel work surface clean in general. Misspelled words, persistent trailing spaces, unnecessary prefixes, inappropriate cases, and nonprinting characters all contribute to a poor initial impression. That isn't even an exhaustive list of the ways your data might be tainted. Bring your sleeves up to your elbows. It's time to do some serious spring cleaning on your Microsoft Excel spreadsheets.

You don't always have control over the format and kind of data you import from a database, text file, or Web page. It's common to have to clean up data before you can examine it. Fortunately, Excel provides a number of functions that might assist you in obtaining data in the format you want. Sometimes the work issimple, and you can rely on a single function to do it for you. Spell Checker, for example, can quickly clear up misspelled words in columns with comments or descriptions. Alternatively, you may use the Eliminate Duplicates dialogue box to swiftly remove duplicate rows.

In other instances, you may need to change one or more columns by converting the imported data into new values using a formula. For example, if you want to eliminate trailing spaces from your data, you may use a formula to create a new column, fill it with data, convert the formulae in the new column to values, and then delete the old column. The following are the fundamental procedures for cleaning data:

☐ Import data from a thirdparty database.
☐ In a separate worksheet, make a backup copy of the original data. ☐ Make that the data isin a tabular format, withcomparable data in each column,

all columns and rows visible, andno blank rows inthe range. Use an Excel table for the best results.

☐ Dothingslikespell-checkingorutilizingtheFindandReplacedialogueboxfirst if you don't need to manipulate columns.
☐ After that, work on activities that need you to manipulate

columns. The following are the general procedures for altering a column:

⬚ Add a new column (B) adjacent to the one that has to be cleaned (A).

⬚ In the new column, fill in the formula (B). A calculated column is automatically formed with data filled down in an Excel table.

⬚ Select the new column (B), copy it, then paste it into the new column as values (B).

⬚ Remove the first column (A), which changes the new column's name to A.

Consider recording a macro or developing code to automate the process of cleaning the same data source on a regular basis. If you don't have the time or resources to automate the process yourself, there are a variety of external add-ins built by thirdparty companies, which are included in the Thirdparty suppliers section.

Data Validation

This is another hidden yet powerful Excel feature. It may be used by an experienced Excel user to create sophisticated Excel dashboardsby assisting you in putting inplace basic errorcheckingmechanisms.Excel'sdatavalidationtoolrestrictswhat ausermay type into a cell. For example, data validation might be used to ensure that a value is between 1 and 6, that a date is within the next 30 days, or that text input is fewer than 25 characters.

Employee records are included in the table below. We want individuals to be forced to input just the departments listed on the left side of the table. In fact, we want them to be able to quickly access a pre-populated dropdown list and choose a department from the possibilities. Choose the cells to which this feature should be applied, then go to the Data menu and select Data.

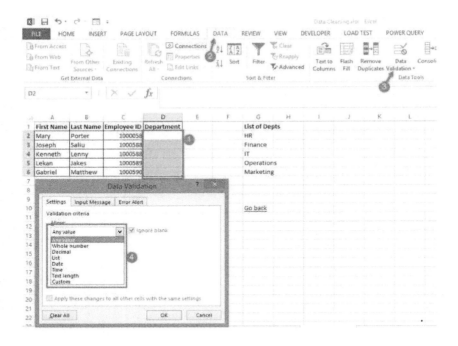

You'll see that there are a lot of alternatives to choose from.

1. Any Value. This is the default setting, and it's the same as having no data validation at all. Any value may be entered into the cell by the user.

2. A complete number. This requires the user to only whole input numbers as numeric values. The user will get an error if he inputs a text or decimal value. If you don't sell fractions of your items, this might be useful on an invoice sheet for the fields that store the order quantity.

3. The decimal system. The user is forced to input a whole integer or a decimal value. A decimal with zeros after the decimal point is the same asa full number. This might be used in a financial model sheet for storing growth assumptions, currency rates, and risk premiums.

4. Make a list. This is the one we're most curious about. It allows us to restrict cell entries to a set of choices. This will be used in the

next example.

5. Make a date. The user is compelled to submit a valid date.

6. The passage of time. The user is compelled to input a genuine time.

7. Text Length. The user may input any value as long as the character length does not exceed the value indicated here. It's useful for fields that store phone numbers; you may wish to restrict entries to the +2348123456789 14-character format.

8. Custom.You want to restrict the cell input to something less traditionaland not covered by the other choices, as the name implies.

Chapter 7: How to Format Data in MS Excel 2022

Format Based on Cell Type

As you already know, Excel spreadsheets will contain a wide range of details, from plain text to complicated formulas. These spreadsheets will grow in complexity and be used to make critical decisions.

It's not all about rendering Excel spreadsheets "attractive." It's just about adding significance to the built-in models. A spreadsheet consumer should be able to take a look at a cell and recognize it without needing to look at each and every calculation. Above everything, styles must be continuously incorporated. When you're using a calculation, one suggestion is to use yellow coloring. This informs the consumer that the value of the cell can adjust depending on the values of other cells.

Format and Data cells:

Enhancing a worksheet's graphic presentation is an essential move toward making it a helpful method because you or your colleagues to use it while making important decisions. When spreadsheets include only currency results, there are agreed to technical formatting requirements. The following Excel Formatting Guidelines would be included in this lesson. When both numbers are in yen, the first figure shows about using accounting number type. The Accounting format can only be used with the first row of details and the totals. The rest of the information should be formatted in a Comma layout. Just above the number in the total lines, there must also be a Top Border. If all of the numbers contain quarters, all of the details must be formatted with two decimal points.

Formatting Instructions (used when both currency and non-currency are reflected in a worksheet). Units and Dollar Amounts on the Same Worksheet in Excel Workbooks without a Documentation sheet include a three-line title: Name of the company, Report Type, and Date When combining units and dollars tables, use the Accounting Number method ($ to format the whole dollar list. If the currency sums are entire pounds, no cents, there are no decimals. Remember to use a spellchecker. Before copying or submitting, print a preview. Do the conclusions make sense after proofreading common sense? Make sure the worksheet is presented in a competent manner.

Your Excel spreadsheet would most likely include both currency and non-currency prices. If that's the case, you'll want to take the steps shown in the diagram:

Change the Font

Per workbook has a specific theme. Per theme comes with a font collection that includes a heading and body font. The headings font will be used to format the body font, and headings will be used to format the body of your workbook. The headings and body fonts used for your workbook's theme are mentioned in the Theme Fonts portion. Adjust the font collection used for the theme if you choose to change the default fonts in your workbook.

All Fonts shows you a rundown of all the fonts that are installed on your device and that you can use. Excel shows every text you've chosen in the font when you run the mouse pointer over it. This is referred to as a "live preview." To use a font, press the name of the font.

How to Change the Font?

1. Choose the cells in which you want to modify the font.

2. Just choose the Home tab.

3. In the Font community, click the arrow next to the Fonts box. A font gallery exists.

4. Drag the mouse cursor over the font list. Excel offers a real-time demo.

5. Choose the font you like by clicking its name. The font is applied to the chosen text in Excel data.

How do I change a theme's font?

The headings and body fonts in Excel are the main theme's fonts until you alter them. To alter the fonts in the style, go to 1) Just choose the Page Layout tab from the drop-down menu. 2) In the Themes group, press Fonts, and then choose the font range you need from the gallery that exists.

You may also make your own font collection. 1) Choose the Page Layout tab from the drop-down menu. 2) In the Themes group, choose Fonts. 3) Choose to Customize Fonts from the drop-down menu. The dialogue box for creating new theme fonts appears. 4) pick a heading font by clicking the drop-down next to the Heading font area. 5) Pick a body font by clicking the down arrow next to the Body Font area. 6) Simply type you want to assign your font collection in the Name area. 7) Save the file. Your font collection is generated by Excel. Your font collection will now display in the Custom portion when you press the Fonts tab.

Change the Font Size

You should adjust the font size in Excel. You might, for example, render a section of your worksheet more significant to draw attention to it or make it smaller to accommodate more details on a printed screen. The size of a font is calculated in points. A point is 1/72 of an inch, which ensures there are 72 points in an inch. A font size could be 9 points, 12 points, 26 points, or 127 points; for example—the bigger the font, the larger the point size.

To adjust the font size, use the following methods: Choose a scale from the Font Size box's drop-down menu, or use the Develop Font or Shrinking Font buttons. The font size is increased by pressing the Grow Font tab. The Shrinking Font button reduces the scale of the font.

Just use font and size Drop-Down Menu to adjust the font size.

1. Find the data with the font size you wish to modify and choose it.

2. Just choose the Home tab.

3. In the Font community, select the down-arrow next to the Font Size box.

4. Choose the desired font size. The font size in Excel is changed.

B	C	D	E
Results ⟶ **Widget Sales**			
	January	February	March
Region 1	4,400	1,200	4,000
Region 2	1,200	1,100	3,300

Use the Grow Font Button

Find the data with the font and size you wish to modify and choose it.

Just choose the Home tab.

In the font of each community, click the Develop Font tab.

Your font size rises with the press. Stop when you've reached the desired size.

Use the Shrink Font Button

Find the data with the font size you wish to modify and choose it.

Just choose the Home tab.

In the Font community, select the Shrink Font tab. The font size decreases with each press. Stop when you've reached the desired size.

Bold, Italicize or Underline

The Excel Ribbon's underline feature has two options: double underline and underline. Two additional alternatives are included in the Format Cells dialogue box: Single Accounting and Double Accounting and Single Accounting. The distinction between an Underline versus a Single Accounting Underline and Underline verses are shown in the example below.

The distinction between a Double Accounting Underline and a Double underline is shown in the example below.

	January		February	
	Widget Sales			
Region 1	$	4,400	$	1,200
Region 2		1,200	Single	
Region 3	Underline	0	Accounting	
Region 4		1,700		2,200
Total	$	8,600	$	6,700

	January		February	
	Widget Sales			
Region 1	$	4,400	$	1,200
Region 2	Double		Double	
Region 3	Underline		Accounting	
Region 4		1,700		2,200
Total	$	8,600	$	6,700

Bold

1. Make a selection of the information you intend to highlight.

2. Just choose the Home tab.

3. In the Font group, click the bold icon. Excel highlights the details you chose.

	Widget Sales		
	January	February	March
Region 1	$ 4,400	$ 1,200	$ 4,000
Region 2	1,200	1,100	3,300
Region 3	1,30 Results 0		3,800
Region 4	1,700 2,200		2,900
Total	$ 8,600	$ 6,700	$ 14,000

Select the details and then press the Highlight button again to delete the bold.

Apply Borders

Borders are useful for segmenting the data and separating it from other parts of your spreadsheet. The border tool in Excel can create many boundaries, but it can be difficult to use at first.

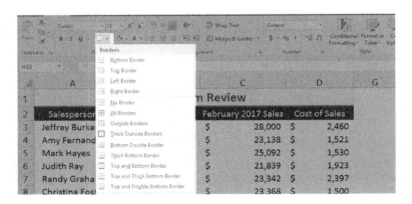

Begin by marking the cells to which you want to add a boundary. Then locate the Borders drop-down list and select one of the pre-installed models.

Border Options Here

From the "Borders" drop-down, you can choose from a number of built-in border choices. Borders can be applied in a variety of ways, as you'll see in the drop-down choices. To add one of these boundary choices to cells, simply click on it. Upper or Double Bottom Borders is one of my main border designs. This is especially useful for financial details with a "grand sum."

Another choice is to alter the border's weight and color. Back to the Borders drop-down panel with the bordered cells picked. Borders may be customized using the Line Type and Line Color options.

Border Added to cells.

The above and below boundaries of my amount are an excellent place to draw attention to specific cells. Thick borders may be used to mark the beginning and bottom of headers columns and also the sum at the bottom of your results.

Use Shading

Shading, also known as fill, is essentially a color applied to the cell's background. To apply shading to a cell, press and highlight the cells you want to shade.

Then, on the Font tab of the Home ribbon, press the cursor next to the color bucket drop-down. To add a color to a cell, choose one of the several color thumbnails. I'll also use the Further Colors alternative to open a full-featured color discovery tool on a regular basis. The easiest way to make text visible is to use light colors.

Shading main rows provides much-needed contrast to the results. You will use shading to illuminate necessary data once more. One suggestion is to use a standard fill centered on the content of the cell, like blue for any "input" areas when you manually type info, as I discussed earlier. Don't go overboard on the coloring. When you apply so much of these to the cells, it detracts from the information contained in the spreadsheet.

Change Alignment

The way the material in a cell is matched to the edges is referred to as alignment. Text may be aligned to the left, middle, or right. In a cell, the material is kept aligned by nature. When working with massive data sets, you will want to experiment with alignment to improve readability.

Alignment, such as centering columns and correct aligning numbers, tends to make a spreadsheet appear much cleaner. The 3 align keys on the Align tab of Excel's Home ribbon may be used to change alignment. You may also change whether the material aligns to the upper, center, or lower of the cell by aligning it vertically.

Understanding Colors

You can adjust the color of data and items in Excel. When you want to adjust color, Excel displays a color gallery divided into three sections: Standard Colors, Theme Colors, and More Colors. This segment will provide you a rundown of the various color choices. You'll learn how to adjust the fill color and font color. You'll learn how to adjust the color of other things in future classes.

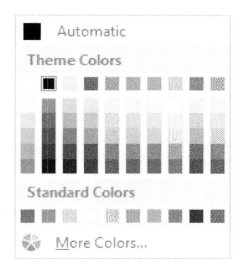

Theme Colors

These colors are a set of colors that you may use in a document or a group of documents. They offer the documents a clear look and feel when used on a daily basis. Per style has a selection of colors associated with it. Do not be concerned if you are unfamiliar with the themes. When it comes to theme colors, keep in mind that if you adjust the design, the data or item color can change as well. If you haven't modified your theme or color scheme, you're using the default themes and color scheme.

Standard Colors

A selection of common colors is known as standard colors. When you choose normal colors, the color of the data or entity does not alter when you change the theme.

More Colors

The Colors dialogue box is opened as you choose More Colors. You may add whatever color you like to the Colors dialogue box. When you choose the More Colors to feature to add a hue, the data or entity color remains the same when you modify the style.

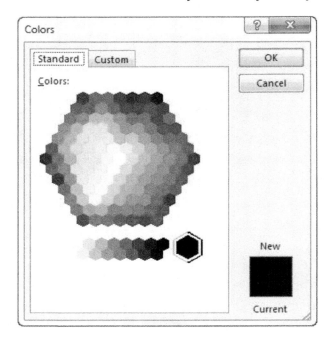

Standard Tab

To pick a color in the Colors dialogue box, go to the Standard tab and click on it.

Custom Tab

Click the Custom tab in the Colors dialogue box to select a color utilizing the RGB or HSL model. The RGB or HSL models are used in many applications. As a result, if you're attempting to fit a color provided by another application, you would like to get one of those versions.

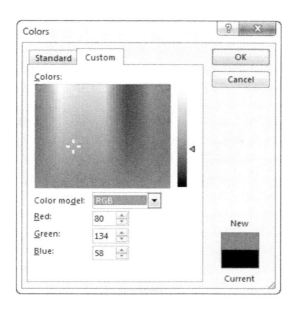

The RGB Model

The letters RGB stand for Red Green Blue. This model utilizes variations of the three main colors, red, green, and blue, to generate all of the colors that a computer monitor will represent. Each one of the primary colors has a 0 to 255 value set. When all three values are set to 0, the result is black; when all three values are set to 255, the result is white. You will create the entire range of colors by changing the Red, Green, and Blue values.

The HSL Model

Hue Saturation Luminosity is an abbreviation for (HSL). A value of 0 to 255 is allocated to each of these components. Hue is a pigment or a color shade. Saturation describes how much grey is added to color; a saturation value of 0 contributes a tonne of grey, whereas a saturation value of 255 adds none. The volume or strength of light present in color is referred to as luminosity; a luminosity setting of 0 equals black, and a luminance setting of 255 equals white. The entire range of colors can be achieved by adjusting the Hue, Luminosity, and Saturation.

Removing Color

To get rid of color, go to the color gallery and pick No Color. The color is removed in Excel. There is no Color choice on the Font Color icon. To restore the default color of files, click the down-arrow next to the Font Colour key and then select Auto.

Change a Background Color (Fill Color)

Excel's default background color is white. You may want to adjust the background color to something different, such as a light brown, at some stage. There is no way to adjust the background color in Excel because it is not a customizable choice. However, there are some workarounds that you might try. One method is to pick all of the cells in the spreadsheet and fill them with a fill pigment. If you wouldn't want the color to print, just pick all of the cells and uncheck the fill color box. The color reduction, printing, and re-application could all be automated with the aid of a macro.

However, there are several disadvantages of such a strategy. First, if conditional formatting uses fill colors, the colors used to fill the cells will interfere with the efficient application of conditional formatting. (Applying conditional formatting to font requirements shouldn't be an issue.)

Another choice is to draw a tiny rectangle in your preferred graphics application that suits the color you want for your backdrop. Use the PNG file format to save the tiny rectangular as a graphics file. Then, under Excel, perform the following steps:

1. Open the ribbon and choose the Page Layout tab.

2. Throughout the Page Setup group, choose the Background tool. The Sheet Background dialogue box appears in Excel 2007 and Excel 2010. The Inserting Pictures screen appears in Excel 2013 and later versions, where you can press the Browse connection to the right of the from the File option. The Sheet Background dialogue box would appear after that.

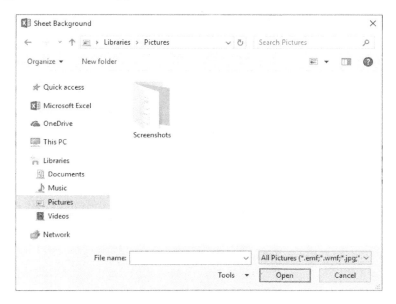

3. Find and pick the graphic picture you generated using the controls in the dialogue box (the small rectangle of color).

4. Select Insert from the drop-down menu.

The graphic picture is put in the background and replicated many times until it completely fills the room. This method has the advantage of not affecting conditional formatting and excluding the context picture from printing.

If you're not using conditional formatting for anything else in your worksheet, you might use it to build your context. Create a cell with the value True in a blank region of your workbook. Instead, for the background color, pick your worksheet and use a conditional method to specify the color. The format will check whether the cell you specified is valid, and if it is, the color is added. The color is not added if the cells are not real. By adjusting the value of a specific cell, you may transform the background color open or closed (for printing).

Styles may be specified used in your worksheet as well. Create two types, one with the ideal background color and the other without. When editing, you can use the colored *type, and when printing, you can use the non-colored style.*

Change the Font Color

Normally, Excel uses black type to represent data. If you're printing on a standard printer, this is acceptable, but several people today have color printers. Additionally, you may like to show details on the computer using various colors. The font color used by Excel may be modified in the following way:

1. Choose the cells where you want to adjust the font color.

2. From the Format menu, choose Cells. The Format Cells dialogue box appears in Excel.

3. Pick the Font tab from the drop-down menu.

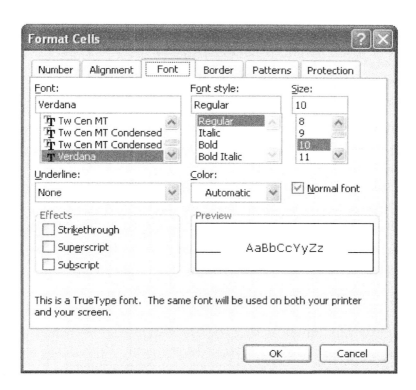

Choose a color for the details in the cells you described in phase 1 from the Color drop-down chart.

Choose OK.

There is another option to adjust the font color, and that could be quicker. The toolbars may be used to adjust the font color in this way.

Choose the cells where you want to adjust the font color.

On the toolbar, click the down arrow on the right-hand side of the Font Colour tool. This shows a color scheme.

Choose the hue you want to use by clicking on it.

The color of the data in the selected cell is updated at this stage. You may have also noted that the Font Color tool's color bar at the lower has shifted. This ensures that all you have to do in the future is pick cells and use the option to adjust the font to the very same color.

Add Borders

A boundary is a line that runs from left to right, top to bottom; Borders may be customized in terms of form and color. There are three methods to add a border: using the Borders tab in the Format Cells Dialog box, drawing a border, or choosing a border alternative from the Borders portion of the Borders Menu.

The Borders Menu's Borders Section

Excel shows a menu of border choices when you press the down arrow next to the Border tab. Pick an alternative from the Boundaries side of the menu to easily add a border. Each choice is explained in the table below.

Border is a menu option in the Borders menu.

Choose the cells you want to work with.

Then choose the Home tab.

Next to one of the Border buttons, click the down arrow. A menu would emerge.

Choose the kind of border you like. The boundary is added by Excel.

Draw a Border There are five choices in the Draw Borders portion of the Borders tab. Each of them is illustrated in the table below.

Option	Function
Make a border	Your mouse pointer is transformed into a pencil. Draws an outer boundary when you drag. You may add a boundary to a cell's edge by clicking it.
Make a border grid	Make a border grid. Turns the cursor pointer into a grid-based pencil. Draws an all-around boundary when you drag. You may add a boundary to a cell's edge by clicking it.
Remove the border	Your mouse pointer is transformed into an eraser. Removes the boundaries from the image. To delete the boundary from a cell, press its side.
Styles of Lines	Line Colour brings up a color picker. Your mouse pointer is transformed into a pencil. Pick a line color from the menu. Draw boundaries with the pencil. You may add a boundary to a cell's edge by clicking it.

The Draw Borders choices operate in an odd way for me. Your mouse pointer changes into a pencil or an eraser when you choose either of these choices. Draw boundaries with the pencil. To delete borders, use the eraser. When you're done drawing or deleting boundaries, press the Esc key. The condition of your mouse cursor will return to usual.

What makes me believe this is odd? So, when you want a Line Color or a Line Style, I assume Excel sets the choice and leaves it at that. It isn't how it works. Excel sets the choice and transforms your mouse pointer into a pencil when you pick a Line Color or Line Style option. You will outline the boundaries with a pencil. If you choose to choose a particular form of a pencil or choose a border from the Borders portion of the menu, you must first click the Esc key and then pick the alternative you choose.

If you've decided on a line color or pattern, you can't change it. If you make a pick from the Borders portion of the Borders menu or draw a border after you've chosen a line color or line type, Excel would use the line color and line style you last selected. The following applies to most keys, but it's especially obvious when it comes to borders. If a down-arrow occurs next to a button, clicking it and then selecting an option from the list or exhibition that appears changes the preference to the button alternative. You don't have to click the down-arrow again to reapply the option; you can simply click the icon.

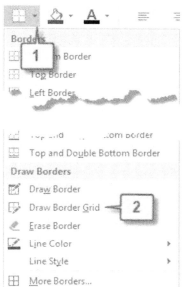

Draw a Border

Beside the Borders button, click the down arrow.

Choose a drawing tool from the drop-down menu. The cursor on your computer becomes a pencil.

To create a border, click and drag.

	C	D	E
Click	Widget Sales		
	January	February	March
Region 1	$ 4,400	Drag 0 $	4,000
Region 2	1,200	1,100	3,300
Region 3	1,300	2,200	3,800
Region 4	1,700	2,200	2,900
Total	$ 8,600	$ 6,700	$ 14,800

The Border tab allows you to design your borders in whatever direction you choose. The choices on the Borders tab are explained as follows: Line Type: Use a line style from the Style box. Select the desired type by clicking on it.

Color: Choose a border color from the Color box. To read all about shades, go here. To apply a color, press the down-arrow beside the Color area and choose the desired color.

Presets: There are multiple toggle buttons in the presets field. A border is applied or removed by clicking a mouse. For e.g., you can add an outside border by clicking the Outline icon, then delete the border by clicking it again.

Note: To delete all borders from your list, click the none tab.

Choose a theme and color, then use the Outlining button to draw a boundary across your range on the upper, lower, left, and right sides.

Inside: Pick a design and color, then press the Inside button to add a border to the upper, lower, left, and right sides of the cells inside your range, but not to the top, bottom, left, or right sides of the selection itself.

Toggle keys can also be used in the boundary region.

Top Border: Pick a design and color, then press the Upper Border button to add a border to the chosen cells' top edges.

On the inside, Horizontal: Pick a design and color, then press the Horizontally Border button to create a horizontal border between the cells you've picked.

Bottom Border: Pick a design and color, then press the Lower Border button to add a border to the cells' bottom edges.

Diagonal Up Border: Choose a design and color, then press the Diagonal Up button to draw a line from the lower-left corner of the chosen cells to the top right corner.

Choose a design and color, then press the Left Borders button to add a border to the left edge of the cells you've picked.

On the inside Vertical: Pick a design and color, then press the Vertical Border button to add a vertical border to any of the cells you've chosen.

Right Border: Pick a design and color, then press the Right Border button to add a border to the chosen cells' right edge.

Diagonal down Border: Choose a design and color, then press the Diagonal Downward button to draw a line from the top left corner of the chosen cells to the lower right.

Text and Cell Alignments

You are able to: ☐ Change vertical cell alignment, ☐ Change horizontal cell alignment, ☐ Change text power ☐ Change the text orientation.

The use of Standard toolbar for aligning numbers and text in cells
You've already found that Excel XP aligns text (labels) to the left and numbers to the right (values). This renders data more readable.

Text and Numbers Alignment by Default You are not obligated to use the default settings. In Excel XP, text and numbers may be aligned to the left, right, or middle. When these alignment forms are added to marks, the distinction between them can be seen in the image below.

147

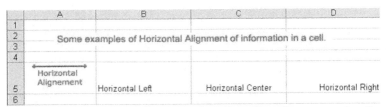

	A	B	C	D
1				
2	Some examples of Horizontal Alignment of information in a cell.			
3				
4				
5	Horizontal Alignement	Horizontal Left	Horizontal Center	Horizontal Right
6				

The left-align, center-align, and right-align keys on the Format toolbar can be used to align text and numbers:

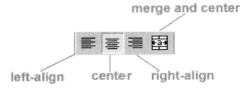

To align numbers or text in a cell:

Choose a cell or a group of cells.

On the Standard toolbar, click a Left-Align, Middle, or a Right-Align keys.

The chosen alignment procedure is applied to the numbers or texts in a cell(s).

Changing horizontal cell alignment We've already learned how to use left-align, center-align, and right-align buttons to align text or numbers on the Standard toolbar. The Align tab of the Format Cells dialogue box may also be used to determine alignment.

The Horizontal segment has a drop-down menu of the same left, middle, and right alignment choices as the image above, plus a few more: *Fill* By repeating the contents for the width of the cell, this covers the cell with the current contents.

Justification If the text in the cell exceeds the cell distance, Explain covers the text in the cell and change the distance inside each line such that both lines are the same width.

Selection could be in the center.

The content of the cell on the far left are centered on the whole set of cells. This command is equivalent to Merge and Center, but the cells are not combined.

To use the Format Cells dialogue box to adjust the horizontal orientation, choose a cell or a set of cells.

⬚ From the menu bar, select Format > Cells.

⬚ Menu Options for Formal and Cells (Alternatively, you can right-click and select Format Cells from the shortcut menu.)

⬚ Select the Alignment button from the drop-down menu.

⬚ The Format Cells Dialog Box's Alignment Tab ⬚ Select a horizontal orientation procedure from the Horizontal drop-down display.

⬚ To add the horizontal orientation to the selected cell, click OK (s).

Changing vertical cell alignment In the same way, as horizontal orientation can be defined in a cell, vertical alignment can be defined as well. Details in a cell can be found at the top, center, or below of the cell as it is vertically aligned. The default position is at the bottom.

To use the Format Cells dialogue box to adjust the vertical orientation,

Choose a cell or a set of cells.

From the menu bar, select Format > Cells.

(You can also right-click and select Format Cells from the shortcut menu.)

This brings up the Format Cells dialogue box.

Select the Alignment button from the drop-down menu.

Find a vertical orientation treatment from the Vertical drop-down menu.

To add the vertical orientation to the selected cell, click OK (s).

Changing text control You may use text control to change how Excel XP displays data in a cell. Wrapped code, shrink to match, and combine cells are the three forms of text power.

	A	B	C	D	E
1		Text Control examples:			
2					
3		This is an example of wrapped text.	————	Wrapped Text	
4					
5		Shrink-to-fit example.	————	Shrink-to-fit	
6					

▢ If the content of a cell is too wide for the column distance, the wrapped text function wraps them over several lines. It also raises the cell's height.

▢ The shrink-to-fit function reduces the size of the text such that it blends into the cell; more the texts in the cell, the shorter it is.

⏹ The Merge and Center buttons on the Standard toolbar can also be used to apply the merge cells function.

Chapter 8: Microsoft Excel 2022 Shortcuts Keys

Using Excel shortcuts or shortcut keys is an often-overlooked way of can efficiency while operating with an Excel model. When used rather than clicking in the toolbar, these shortcut keys execute large functions that greatly improve performance and speed. Consider hitting just two to three keys on the keyboard rather than shifting the hand to the cursor, moving the button, then clicking several times.

There are lots of keyboard Excel shortcuts available to help you get something done in Excel. These shortcuts may be used for a variety of tasks, ranging from basic spreadsheet navigation to formula filling and data grouping.

Excel's basic shortcut terminology Before diving into Excel shortcuts, it's a good idea to go through the basic terminology for the various Excel components.

Either of the several boxes in the Excel spreadsheet is referred to as a cell.

Excel's active cell is the one that is actually chosen. There can be only one functioning cell at any given time.

The active cell, or even a group of cells, is referred to as a selection. If the range contains more than one cell, the active cell will be displayed in white, while the remainder of the selection will be grey.

A column is a collection of vertical cells in Excel that are referred to by letters ranging from A to Z. Excel can repeat letters a second time after column Z. As a result; column AA is the next column after column Z, preceded by column AB.

Text is a type of data that is made up of letters. Text data may also contain numbers. These numbers, on the other hand, must be used in combination with letters or manually set to text.

Numbers are data sets that are mostly made up of numbers. Number type data cannot use characters, unlike text type data, which does.

Numbers are used in combination with a currency marker in currency/accounting info.

Dates are pieces of information that represent a date and/or period. In Excel, dates may be formatted in a variety of ways.

Data of the percentage kind is a subset of numerical data that has been transformed into a percentage. These can be translated back into data of the number type and vice versa. When you convert a percentage to a number, the result is a decimal. Eighty-nine percent, for example, would be converted to 0.89.

You will save time by using the Excel keyboard shortcuts mentioned below. You may either scroll down the collection or use the Index to easily find the section you're looking for.

General Shortcuts Keys

Ask for assistance.	(F1)
Undo the previous activity.	(Ctrl) + (Z)
Repeat the last action.	(F4)
Cut the selected text.	(Ctrl) + (X)
Display the Special Paste.	(Ctrl) + (Alt) + (V)

Display find & replace with the Find tab chosen.	(Ctrl) + (F)
Display find & replace with the Replace tab chosen.	(Ctrl) + (H)
Find the previous match [after initial Find]	(Ctrl) + (Shift) + (F4)
Find the next match [after initial Find]	(Shift) + (F4)
Insert embedded chart.	(Alt) + (F1)
Insert chart on new sheet.	(F11)
Toggle the Auto filter.	(Ctrl) + (Shift) + (L)
Filter Activate.	(Alt) + (↓)
Create table.	(Ctrl) + (T) OR (Ctrl) + (L)
Chose table row.	(Shift) + (Space)
Chose table column.	(Ctrl) + (Space)
Chose table [when the active cell is in table]	(Ctrl) + (A)
Filter for clear slicers.	(Alt) + (C)
Run Spellcheck.	(F7)
Toggle Thesaurus.	(Shift) + (F7)
The Macro dialog box Open.	(Alt) + (F8)

VBA Editor Open.	(Alt) + (F11)
Duplicate text, formula, object.	(Ctrl) + (D)
Select to grid [whilst dragging]	(Alt)
Seen or hidden objects.	(Ctrl) + (6)
The Modify Cell Style dialogue box will appear.	(Alt) + (')
Show the right-click menu.	(Shift) + (F10)
Display the control menu.	(Alt Space)

Number Formatting Shortcuts Keys

General format use	Ctrl + Shift + ~
Number format use	Ctrl + Shift + !
Time format use	Ctrl + Shift + @
Date format use	Ctrl + Shift + #
Currency format use	Ctrl + Shift + $
Percentage format use	Ctrl + Shift + %
Scientific format use	Ctrl + Shift + ^

Navigation Shortcuts Keys

Go/Move one cell right	→

Go/Move one cell left	←
Go/Move one cell up	↑
Go/Move cell down	↓
Go/Move one screen right	Alt + PgDn
Go/Move one screen left	Alt + PgUp
Go/Move one screen up	PgUp
Go/Move one screen down	PgDn
Go/Move to right edge of the data region	Ctrl + →
Go/Move to left edge of the data region	Ctrl + ←
Go/Move to top edge of the data region	Ctrl + ↑
Go/Move to bottom edge of the data region	Ctrl + ↓
Go/Move to beginning of the row	Home
Go/Move to last cell in worksheet that contains data	Ctrl + End
Go/Move to first cell in worksheet	Ctrl + Home
Turn End mode on	End

Selection Shortcuts Keys

Choose/Select the entire row	Shift + Space
Choose/Select the entire column	Ctrl + Space

Choose/Select the current region if the worksheet contains data. Again, press to select the current region & summary rows. Again, press to select the entire worksheet.	Ctrl + A
Expand the selection	Shift + Click
Add non-adjacent cells to selection	Ctrl + Click
Shift/Move right between the non-adjacent selections	Ctrl + Alt + →
Shift/Move left between the non-adjacent selections	Ctrl + Alt + ←
'Add to Selection' mode Toggle	Shift + F8
'Add to Selection' mode Exit	Esc

Entering Data Shortcuts Keys

Enter data & move down	Enter
Enter data & move up	Shift + Enter
Enter data & move right	Tab
Enter data & move left	Shift + Tab
Enter data & stay in same cell	Ctrl + Enter
Enter same data in multiple cells	Enter
Current date Insert	Ctrl +;

Current time Insert	Ctrl + Shift +:
Fill down from cell above	Ctrl + D
Fill right from cell on left	Ctrl + R
Copy formula from cell above (exact copy)	Ctrl + '
Copy value from cell above	Ctrl + Shift + "
Insert hyperlink	Ctrl + K
AutoComplete list Display	Alt + ↓
Flash fill	Ctrl + E

Formatting Shortcuts Keys

Format cells	Ctrl + 1
Display Format Cells with Font tab selected	Ctrl + Shift + F
Bold – Add or remove	Ctrl + B
Italics – Add or remove	Ctrl + I
Underscore – Add or remove	Ctrl + U
Strikethrough – Add or remove	Ctrl + 5
Centre Align	Alt + H, A C
Left Align	Alt + H, A L
Right Align	Alt + H, A R

Indent	Alt + H, 6
Indent Remove	Alt + H, 5
Text Wrap	Alt + H, W
Top Align	Alt + H, A T
Middle Align	Alt + H, A M
Bottom Align	Alt + H, A B
Increase one step font size	Alt + H, F G
Decrease one step font size	Alt + H, F K

Formulas Shortcuts Keys

Start by entering a formula.	= OR +
Toggled (in cell edit mode) relative & absolute references	(F4)
The Insert Function Dialog Box would display.	(Shift) + (F3)
Auto sum	(Alt) + (=)
Switch on and off the display of formulas.	(Ctrl) + (`)
Insert arguments to the function.	(Ctrl) + (Shift) + (A)
Filled in the array formula.	(Ctrl) + (Shift) + (Enter)

Worksheets to calculate	(F9)
Calculate the active worksheet (operational)	(Shift) + (F9)
Force all worksheets to be calculated	(Ctrl) + (Alt) + (F9)
(in cell edit mode) evaluate part formula	(F9)
The formula bar expanded or collapsed.	(Ctrl) + (Shift) + U)
Dialog box for feature arguments to be displayed	(Ctrl) + (A)
Open the Name Manager application.	(Ctrl) + (F3)
In rows, columns create name from values	(Ctrl) + (Shift) + (F3)
Into the formula, Paste the name	(F3)
Auto-complete accept feature	(Tab)

Conclusion

Thank you for reading this book. Microsoft Excel is database software for recording, manipulating, and storing numeric data. In Excel, the ribbon is used to access different commands. The options dialog window allows you to configure a variety of features, such as the ribbon, formulas, proofing, and saving.

Excel's main advantage is that it allows for speedy data input. MS Excel features a Ribbon interface, which is a collection of instructions that may be used to do particular tasks, as opposed to other data entering and analysis techniques. The ribbon is divided into tabs, each of which has a number of command groups and keys that go with it. You may quickly choose instructions and perform operations by tapping the appropriate tab.

Excel has a computer language called VBA [Visual Basic for Applications] associated with it. Really good exponents of Excel use VBA all the time. If you wish to master it, you must know the basics of formulas and functions inside and out. This book has thoroughly covered many of those basics.

Excel allows users to analyze, organize, and analyze quantitative data, enabling managers and senior staff to make key choices that might affect the firm with the knowledge they need. Employees that are taught sophisticated Excel functions will be able to present their data more effectively to senior management. It's also a necessary talent for individuals who want to work their way to the top. Employees and employers alike can benefit from superior Excel knowledge.

Because Excel is part of the Microsoft Office suite, it may be able to connect with other apps in the suite. For example, you may need to move data from Excel to MS Access or vice versa. Excel is a flexible platform that can be used both at home and at work.

The most popular platform for analyzing data, making charts and presentations, and connecting with strong tools for visual dashboards and business intelligence processes will continue to remain Microsoft Excel.

Microsoft Excel 2022 brings together detailed and concise information on using all aspects of the latest and most relevant version of Microsoft Excel.

Even better, mastering advanced Excel can help you improve the efficiency of your computations. Calculations that have to be repeated take time, particularly when you have to doublecheck your results. You may make more sophisticated computations using sophisticated Excel features. Once you've typed your formula and programmed your set command, the software will do the calculations for you, saving up your time for other chores and guaranteeing that you get correct results the first time.

Being an excel expert not only ensures your job stability but also allows you to grow your career. Being more efficient, more educated, and knowledgeable in your work tasks can help you become more valuable to the firm. That is what advanced Excel training can deliver. To prevent being replaced by fresher workers with a more advanced skill set, employees should continuously look for methods to boost their value to the organization. To remain on top of your game and put yourself up for greater security and development, you must learn and master new talents.

Excel is commonly used for data organization and financial reporting. It is seen in both corporate functions and for businesses of all sizes. Excel is used for accountants, investment managers, consultants, and individuals in all aspects of financial careers to fulfil their everyday tasks.

Excel is often unavoidable in marketing, but with the tips mentioned above, it doesn't have to be so intimidating. Practice makes perfect, as they say. These formulae, shortcuts, and methods will become second nature the more you utilize them.

Good luck

Printed in Great Britain
by Amazon

80220704R00098